Contents

Dedicated to my wife, Soyeon,
who has been with me through all the
incredible ups and downs of this exciting journey.
And to our family and friends.
Thank you and cheers!

Foreword

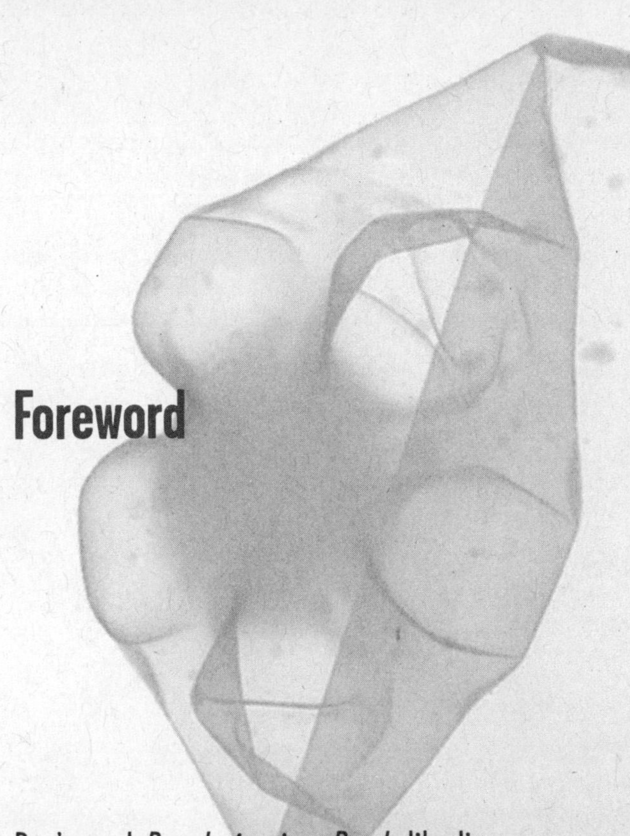

Don't read *Revolution in a Bottle* like literature or a case study. This is not a ripe "I-did-it-my-way" vanity by someone who lucked out and made a lot of money. This is an overture to the shadow of modernity, a pulsing story of incipient commerce that is the birth of a new asset class: the unrecyclable industry. Tom Szaky invented a new category of business, a company functioning like a detritivore that fractions industrial waste into ingenious new products that feed retail environments. Szaky is an entrepreneurial Princeton dropout who never saw a waste problem he couldn't remedy. The problem he solves is the incalculable volume of garbage generated by factories because of the badly designed take-make-waste system of industrial civilization. His paradigm is simple: unwanted molecules of industry equal feedstock for TerraCycle.

There are several things to do with waste. Throw it away and hope nature takes care of it. Incinerate it so that the molecules go someplace else, and hope nature takes care of it. Recycle it and when it is ultimately thrown away, hope nature takes care of it. Tom's method: pay me to take the waste away and let our people redesign it into something your customers will buy. Szaky's first product set the gold standard for waste: the shipping carton is garbage, the bottles are soda pop throwaways, the content is worm poop made from kitchen waste, and maybe, just maybe, this is the first time a Pepsi bottle contained something of value. In the trade, TerraCycle's worm poop in a bottle is known as upcycling. Take a material and make it more valuable than its first incarnation.

In the TerraCycle warehouse, Mylar overprints for shade-grown coffee bags cover Starbucks journals. Kool-Aid packets become pencil holders for Target. TerraCycle makes Oreo Messenger Bags, Capri Sun Tote Bags, Clif Bar backpacks and newspaper pencils galore. You don't merely have a corporate logo on your knapsack, you are a walking cookie package. Szaky's products would have destroyed Andy Warhol's career in a prior decade. The number of SKUs climbs with every season. Szaky's business is like a delectable group of edible toadstools growing out of the muck.

This mash-up of consumerism and material cycling has extensive commercial implications. Conceivably, TerraCycle could be the first company that has negative cost of goods. Competitors have already taken notice. TerraCycle is taking the shadow side of industrial practices and bringing them back to light as products other companies pay them to produce. The long-term implications are even more mind-boggling. What if most industrial waste streams are banned from landfills and incinerators, as is becoming the case in Europe and Japan? Who are you going to call? In other words, rather than an outlet for overruns and abandoned SKUs, TerraCycle could become an integral part of product planning for the dozens of Fortune 500 companies, including the ones it already serves. What happens then is a symbiotic relationship, which is exactly what a detritivore has with its environment. It munches the waste from a tree and feeds the tree, which feeds the detritivore, and we call that relationship life, an extensive integration of mutualism where all parties benefit.

The impression you get from Szaky is an unabashed, bring-it-on, joyful celebration of the discarded, marginal, and hidden. When you see the lineup of iconic corporate logos emblazoning the product line, there is not a trace of doubt in Szaky. He looks unbelievingly at those who question his all-out effort to place his goods in Wal-Mart, Target, and Home Depot. He is proud of his wares, that they are inexpensive and available to every American pocketbook. Every item would otherwise be burned or buried by now. Instead of landfill, his TerraCycle pencil holders contain TerraCycle pencils in TerraCycle knapsacks protected by TerraCycle umbrellas held by children whose clothes were washed in green TerraCycle cleaners packaged in sixty-four-ounce soda bottles.

Waste has negative value in economic terms. In nature, waste is manna, and is becoming gold in the world of Tom Szaky. Alchemy is the story here. It is the magic of passion, brilliance, and persistence coupled with the belief that we are our litter's keeper. For every wannabe green entrepreneur reading this book, note that Szaky's original business knowledge couldn't fill a thimble. But his business imagination filled the earth. This is rare. His vision benefits the earth, the poor, and the giant corporations at the same time. Such an idea will attract all the business knowledge it needs and create its own universe of intelligence. Eventually it becomes the new conventional wisdom and students will study it in school and books, but by then there will be new Szakys outraging the norms. In a world where our collective prospects seem bleak if not absent, the best thing we can do is create a livable future, proving that there is no such thing as inconsequential action. Tom is focused on every discarded wrapper, bottle, mill end, and overrun. The grandness of this vision is grounded in minutia. All 10 septillion detritivores that keep our soils and waters fertile, nourished, and clean are cheering Szaky on. And so should we.

—**PAUL HAWKEN**
Coauthor of *Natural Capitalism*
and author of *Blessed Unrest*

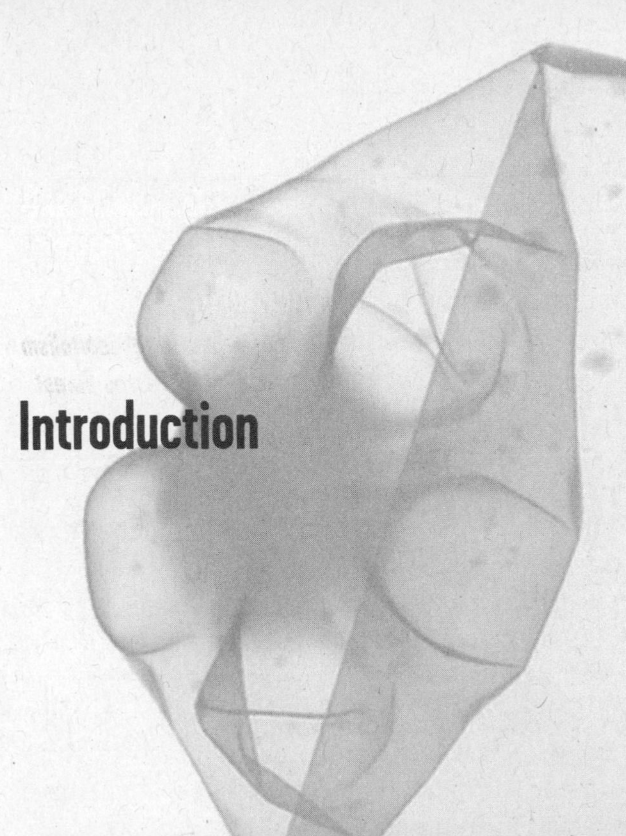

Introduction

In 2002, I dropped out of Princeton University to found TerraCycle, a company that makes products from waste and packages them in waste. It started with turning garbage into worm poop, liquefying it, then packaging the stuff directly in used soda bottles, creating TerraCycle Plant Food. In the five years since, TerraCycle's sales have more than doubled every year. Our more than one hundred products are selectively available in every North American Home Depot, Target, Walgreens, Office Max, Kroger, Whole Foods, and Wal-Mart store, as well as in more than five thousand other locations. We are also under exclusive contract with some of the world's largest brands to collect, with the engagement of millions of individuals, their unrecyclable packaging waste. We then use that waste packaging to make new "upcycled" products.

In the chapters ahead, I share with you a rather graphic account of how we built TerraCycle over the past six years. Some of what follows is anecdotal; it's been a wild ride and

I hope you enjoy the front-row seat. Interspersed with these accounts are my reflections as a green entrepreneur and some of my philosophies about eco-capitalism. I don't believe that every lesson I've learned or insight I've applied is universal; I do hope that my experiences and methodologies will be useful to people who choose to participate in new ventures, particularly those that reduce the huge amount of waste involved in how goods are produced and exchanged on this planet.

In many ways, what follows are lessons I learned on the job as an untrained and highly instinctual entrepreneur. TerraCycle taught me extreme forms of bootstrapping, and many of the innovations for which we are known were responses to failures of initial attempts in packaging, marketing, product development, and even investor pitches. For me, the key to our success was having one big idea—making the greenest, most affordable and effective products from waste—and holding firmly to it. As you will see, there were numerous times when, for example, to attract investment, we might have compromised our environmental commitments, but if we did, TerraCycle would have ended up like one of many companies, rather than in a league of its own. We let the idea of our company—producing a range of green products made from and packaged in waste without charging a premium for them—live and grow within us. Not only did that commitment distinguish us with our immediate customers (large retail companies), end consumers, local and national press, and the brands that are sponsored waste partners, it also gave us cost advantages over other companies producing green products.

I was fortunate to build TerraCycle during a perfect storm of economic, consumer, and industry pressures for cheaper and better green products. I have no doubt that it would have been impossible to create this company a decade earlier. But even within this fertile environment, I firmly believe TerraCycle has been successful because we consistently chose (and were often forced by circumstance) to think outside the box and to challenge mainstream convention. It wasn't just that I knew green products would only succeed with mainstream consumers if they are sold at par with conventional products: In the beginning, we took what looked like extreme green pathways (like packaging our liquid fertilizer in used soda bottles) because we couldn't afford to buy new bottles in bulk. Ultimately, though, our best innovations came from applying out-of-the-box thinking to new circumstances and waste streams.

TerraCycle would never have succeeded if we had started it in another country. America is a land of unique opportunity, and it happens to produce disproportionate amounts of waste. A maverick with a big idea can go further in America than in any other country, and in our case, we were able to tap into the profound desire of millions of Americans to do good, if given the right vehicles and incentives. We already have millions of people, young and old, enthusiastically collecting hundreds of millions of juice pouches and cookie wrappers that would otherwise go to landfills; their incentive is to do the right thing and to generate modest contributions to their designated charities. With its many sizable challenges, America offers unique hope and possibility. As someone not born here, I am grateful to America for allowing me to incubate TerraCycle in its uniquely fertile soil.

In addition to holding firm our big idea, I have always seen the importance of scale and thus of taking TerraCycle big. The one and only clear way to achieve scale as a consumer products company in America is to sell through big-box retailers. As you will read about in the chapters that follow, I have long argued that if environmentally driven businesses are going to move beyond a marginal presence in the market, they must offer the greenest options in the stores that sell over 80 percent of the products in America. And most people, certainly those who shop at Wal-Mart, aren't generally as focused on green in their product choices as are shoppers at Whole Foods. For me, eco-capitalism is about seeking economic and environmental synergies, and in TerraCycle's case the application of this concept is to derive value from waste and to pass on those savings to the retailer and consumer. We have a long way to go to prefect our own model, but I think we have paved a path that will hopefully inspire you and others.

As I think over the roller coaster of TerraCycle's early history, which you are about to read, I can see that it would have been impossible to predict or plan how to develop TerraCycle so that it would make it to the place where it stands today. The trick was to be ever vigilant in seeking opportunities, and to be ready to jump on them if they felt right inside and consistent with our core mission, even before they could be well thought out. And I have learned, by picking up the shovel (when we made our first batches of worm poop) and actually working the iron and sewing machine as we made our prototype upcycled materials and bags, that I could ground an idea in real time and shortcut speculation about the hypothetical.

As you will see, I almost lost control of TerraCycle several times. In each case, friends and angels have shown up at what appeared to be the darkest of moments. Luck and epiphanies were important to TerraCycle's early survival and, over time, to our success. TerraCycle's growth and success was made possible by the hard work, imagination, and profound commitments of so many people to whom I will forever be grateful. And I truly believe that the company, like the ideas that inspire and guide it, has a life of its own. I'm thrilled to share the first six years of TerraCycle's story with you. I hope you will share my excitement about its future.

—TOM SZAKY
Trenton, New Jersey
November 2008

CHAPTER 1

Up to My Neck

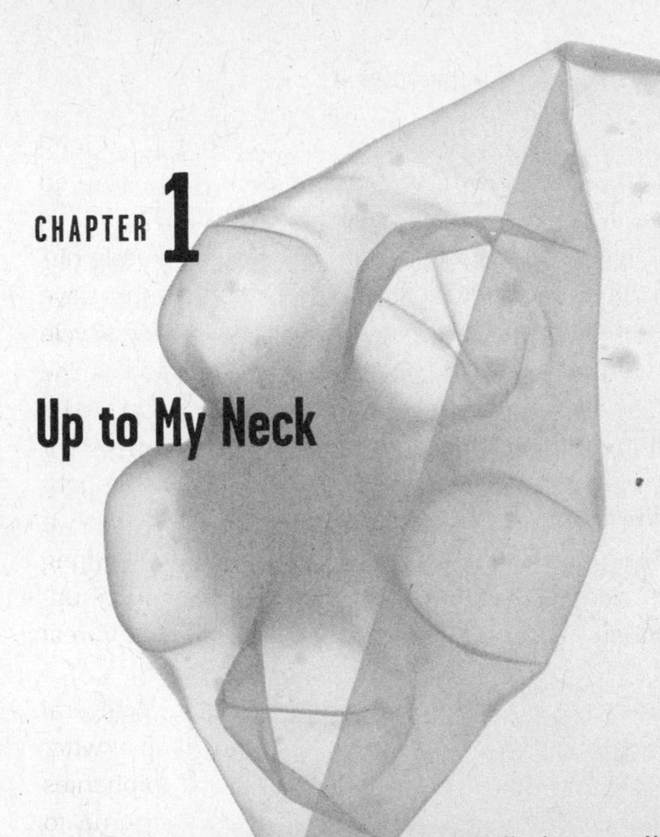

September 10, 2001, I landed in—of all places—New Jersey! I know what you're thinking, and once I landed so was I. I never knew where Princeton University was and was happy enough to get in, so I never bothered finding out until I looked at my plane ticket.

New Jersey is a gigantic suburb in between New York City and Philadelphia. It officially calls itself "the Garden State" and is unofficially called "the garbage state." If you've ever watched an episode of *The Sopranos* you'll know just how famous Jersey is for its waste-management business.

By the end of freshman year you'd expect that I would have been pumped to leave New Jersey and go back to Canada for the summer, or go to New York City to work at an internship. Instead I decided to stay on campus and start a company . . . a worm-poop company. For reasons you will soon find out, for almost the whole of my freshman year I had been fascinated with the commercial potential of fairly ordinary earthworms—red wigglers, *Eisenia fetida*—which thrive on ordinary household garbage. They are voracious consumers of organic waste of all kinds and their principal by-product, just like all animals' (even us humans), is, naturally, poop (worm castings, in the language of the trade). And the best part: worm poop makes a terrific fertilizer.

Somehow, this combination of garbage, worms, and worm-poop fertilizer struck me as a revolutionary business model. People would pay me to take away their garbage, I figured, the worms would eat it and make poop, and I would box up the poop and sell it. That is to say, the cost of my raw materials was negative (people paid me), my employees worked for free (or for room and board, so to speak), and what they poop people would also pay for. I would make money on both ends.

And I really did need to make some money. Partly because I was in debt above my ears as a result of my new venture. I never dreamt of being filthy rich—I don't particularly care about elegant clothes or palatial mansions or sleek sports cars. But I knew that this new business model wouldn't work unless it could work on the most basic principle of business—making profit.

So during freshman year, and despite numerous ups and downs, my friend Jon Beyer and I (with the help of some others) had worked up a business plan, scraped together the cost of a machine that could house millions of worms and collect their poop, and convinced the university to give us the waste from one of the dining halls on campus.

The first day of that hot, sticky summer in New Jersey there I was, staring at a mountain of garbage from one of Princeton's dining halls.

Unfortunately, Jon had returned to Maryland to work as a waiter over the summer. That reduced the staff of TerraCycle by 50 percent. Luckily, I had convinced a senior named Noemi Millman to join us. I'd met Noemi when I worked with a campus theater group, designing posters for their productions. She was a theater major and didn't really have any firm plans for that summer. I convinced her to join TerraCycle without letting on that her job description included shoveling garbage.

We were waiting for Harry. Harry Windle was the inventor and builder of the worm-compost machine that I had bought and was on his way from Florida to deliver it. He was even giving it to us for half price: $20,000. The university had let us use a small area pretty far down the hill for a work site, a little patch of beaten-down grass and dirt perfect for our minimal needs. In preparation for the arrival of the worm gin, Noemi and I had brought the crucial tools of our trade as worm farmers: a 1985 Rent-A-Wreck Ford pickup—rusty black, missing a headlight as well as a rearview mirror—some shovels, and a wood chipper.

We needed the wood chipper because worms will eat just about anything that's organic and fresh, but they don't eat it very efficiently if it's still in large chunks. They would work much better if their food was ground up into a homogeneous sludge. The plan was to drive to the dining hall, load the buckets into our truck, and drive them out to the site. Once there, we'd open them up and start shoveling their contents into the wood chipper. Then we'd simply transfer the resulting sludge, of chopped maggots and rotting food, onto the worm gin's conveyor belt, where it would enter the machine and feed the worms.

All we needed now was Harry Windle and his worm gin. Harry was late. And Princeton had been collecting food waste for us from the dining hall for a week, so that we'd really be able to hit the ground running. I didn't lose confidence, though—I still owed him $10,000 for the gin. He'd built it (and I owed him); he would come.

The Wilcox Dining Hall people had started to bug us about removing those barrels of waste they had been collecting. Understandably. It had been a hot week, and the contents of those barrels weren't getting any fresher.

Finally, two days after we were supposed to start, a massive red F-350 pickup truck crashed onto Washington Road, bearing our unassembled worm gin. After it screeched to a stop in front of us, Harry climbed out carrying his gallon jug of coffee and said, "Wheah d'ya wannit?"

Harry was a tall, fifty-year-old man from the swamps of Gainesville, Florida. A man who had done everything from raising hundreds of bulldogs to buying a cow (Betsy) so that he didn't have to mow his own grass and inventing automatic worm-poop machines. Harry stayed with us for a week to help set up the worm gin and get it going (and to get his money). When it was assembled, the worm gin was a thing of beauty: Imagine a Christmas tree built with very wide conveyer belts, six on each side of the "trunk," standing about fifteen feet high and twenty wide. The worms lived on the angled belts, partaking of the snowfall of garbage that would fall from a central hopper that sat on top.

Each conveyor belt moved away from the center very, very slowly—about an inch every five hours. The idea was that the worms would move up toward the food (away from their poop, since we know all animals, including us, don't like hanging out in their own poop) while the conveyor belt was moving down and away from the center—carrying the worm poop along. When the worm poop reached the bottom of the belt, it would simply fall into some black plastic tubs. Simple.

There were two other parts to the worm gin, and they were actually the beginning and end of the whole process. The first part was a large revolving drum, which would cook the garbage to make it even easier for the worms to eat. It was a silver octagonal tube, about twelve feet long by six feet high, which acted as a super composter. The other component was the screener, another long silver tube, which separated the worm poop from anything else (including any unfortunate worms that didn't crawl fast enough). There were always some items in the garbage that the worms would not eat or at least didn't get around to eating.

We spent most of the day putting together these units. With the sun setting, Harry pulled out a bunch of bulky burlap sacks. Bulky, but not really heavy. These were our worms' travel cases. Inside were a million red wigglers, cushioned from the journey's jolting by shredded paper. When Harry opened up the first one, I wasn't quite sure what I was looking at. Inside, mixed with the paper, were what looked like red grapefruits, except that they were quivering. It turns out that when worms are frightened they clump together and curl themselves up into balls. Harry assured us that once they were settled into the worm gin they would be perfectly fine.

To make them comfortable, and easier to spread into the gin, we mixed them with cow manure (also provided by Harry, courtesy of his lawn mower, Betsy) and loaded them into the central hopper. Gradually, they started to distribute themselves along the conveyor belts.

By that time it was 11:00 p.m., and unfortunately Harry's two-day delay meant that the garbage was stacked up behind us and we needed to get it as soon as possible. As Noemi and I drove across campus in the rattletrap truck, I tried to keep her excited about the big picture—telling her how neat it was to be starting a new business, what a huge effect we could have on the environment if the business model worked, and anything else I could think of.

In fact I was trying to encourage myself as much as Noemi. I was sick to my stomach about the debt! I had spent many sleepless nights trying to figure out exactly how the business would work. I was terrified that the project would fail and I would have to pay the money back. I imagined spending three years in my personal equivalent of the gulag: wearing a suit at an investment bank. My own excitement had some powerful competition from plain old fear—the worm project could not fail. Failure was no longer an option.

Wilcox Dining Hall had accumulated a dozen fifty-five-gallon barrels—the size of standard oil drums—full of what is known within the composting biz as "postconsumer food waste." The term rolls easily off the tongue, but of course there is no such thing as sanitary, inoffensive garbage. These drums were full of rotting cafeteria leftovers that not even hungry college students were interested in: slop composed of everything from half-eaten sausages to last Tuesday's tuna casserole, coffee grounds and cooking oil, eggshells, and all the noxious, unidentifiable sludge in between. All mashed down by its own weight and gradually turning liquid. And not only were we facing a virtual mountain of this slurry, but it had been sitting out in the hot sun putrefying for ten days before we got our hands on it.

In the eerie half-light of our truck's headlights and the campus streetlights, we stared loading the truck. We had a piece of plywood from Home Depot, which we used as a makeshift ramp to push the barrels up and into the bed. Noemi was game, but those puppies weighed upwards of 150 pounds. We shoved and grappled and dragged a couple of barrels into the truck and decided that would be enough for a start. We needed to get the worms working so we headed back to the site.

As we drove up, the low rumble of thunder alerted us to the gathering clouds in the dark sky. Noemi glared at me as if to say, "I can't believe you actually convinced me to do this." We both knew things were about to get ugly.

I glanced at the worm gin, shiny and new and gleaming, waiting to fulfill its destiny. I smiled at Noemi encouragingly and we put on gloves. As carefully as I could, I lifted the lid off the first barrel.

That hot June night, I learned something that I would rather have lived my whole life without knowing. I learned that the combination of heat, moisture, and waste is the perfect environment for decomposition. Not only that, it forms the ideal breeding ground for maggots. Ten days gave them the chance to mature.

So, upon removing the lid from that first barrel, I was greeted by the most rancid natural odor I have ever had the misfortune of encountering. It was infinitely worse than any smell—feces or vomit or decay—that you could possibly imagine and was complemented by an army of writhing maggots that made it appear as if the moldering sludge was actually alive.

And it was all mine.

"Just breathe through your mouth," I gasped, throwing Noemi a shovel.

Things quickly went from bad to worse. As if the fact that we were shoveling this shit wasn't horrific enough, the wood chipper had been designed to grind up dry dead wood—not the greasy cafeteria leftovers of privileged undergraduates. The sludge that had been brewing in those garbage cans proved to be a nightmare for the chipper. Every ten minutes or so it would clog. Of course, the only way to unclog the machine was to reach deep down into it and scrape out, by hand, the garbage that had clogged its teeth. And since the teeth were slightly more than an arm's length away, we almost always got just a little bit of that oh-so-pleasant glop on our faces. Once the machine was finally cleared, we'd transfer the vile pulp onto the conveyor belt leading into the cooking drum and start all over again with a new barrel of garbage. And then go back to Wilcox for two more barrels.

At midnight, it began to drizzle.

We were heaving two more barrels into the truck when we were suddenly caught in a swirl of glaring flashlights. An authoritative voice asked, "Just what are you doing here?"

It took me a minute to be able to piece together an explanation that any reasonable person—much less the campus police—would find acceptable. *We're stealing garbage* wasn't really accurate, and certainly wouldn't endear me to the cops. Finally, I was able to convince them of the truth, that the university had authorized us to dispose of the waste from the dining hall. After a lot of yes-sirring and nodding, we went back to the job.

By the time we'd dispatched the police, the rain was coming down in sheets. After a while, Noemi and I were too exhausted and stunned to talk to each other anymore. Harry was long gone. The whole odious process went on late into the night. Understandably, by our sixth and final trip Noemi was already near the end of her rope. It was after two thirty in the morning when, on the slippery wooden plank we'd devised for loading the pickup, the last barrel fell over, spilling the putrid, maggot-infested swill all over her legs and feet.

Noemi staggered a few steps, puked, and quit.

CHAPTER 2

Praise to Marley, Let the Enlightenment Begin

The six months between starting Princeton and shoveling food waste had obviously required some major change on my part. I guess I was used to it; my life had actually begun with major turmoil. I was born in 1982 in Budapest, Hungary, when it was still a rock-solid communist stronghold. My parents were doctors, but because they refused to join the Communist Party, a neighbor ratted us out and the secret service confiscated our passports. My dad, mom, aunt, grandfather, and I all lived together in a tiny apartment. We had no money; even though they were doctors, my parents made the same as the guy who pushed the elevator buttons in our building (rock on, communism!).

Life in Hungary in the late 1980s was no picnic even in the best of times, but then in April of 1986 the nuclear reactor in Chernobyl blew up. This epic environmental disaster greatly compromised the economy and food supply of all Eastern European nations, since they could no longer export food for fear of contamination. Tremendous political instability descended on the region in an instant. Somehow my parents got our passports back, and at age four I was suddenly told we were leaving our home. We escaped that night with not much more than the clothes on our backs.

We made it to Belgium and stayed there for three months, then moved on to Holland, where we lived for over a year with a professor my parents had met at a conference. America wouldn't give us refugee status, but Canada did, so we emigrated there. I landed in Canada in 1987, and we moved into my mother's uncle's basement. Eventually, we ended up in Scarborough, a fairly sketchy part of Toronto.

Though both my parents had been respected physicians in Hungary, they were forced to redo all their training in order to be able to practice medicine in Canada, beginning with their internships. But despite the fact that my family basically had to start over from scratch, I grew up happily in Toronto, attending elementary school there and, eventually, Upper Canada College (UCC), one of the top all-boys private high schools in the country.

At UCC my best friends opened my eyes to the world of possibilities afforded by entrepreneurship. Jake Cohl's dad, Michael, had come from a nice middle-class family, worked his way into the concert business, and become the largest concert promoter in the history of rock and roll. Anthony Green's father, Don, cofounded ROOTS clothing. Neither of them finished college; both had simply followed their dreams and accomplished amazing things.

Until then, I'd figured people who had money pretty much had it from day one and then kept it to themselves while the rest of us worked for a living and never got to be very rich at all. Before I met Michael and Don and saw firsthand how they lived, I'd never imagined that such a thing was possible. Suddenly, success on a huge scale was an option for me, too!

When I was around fourteen, I figured out how to design Web sites. It never dawned on me that I should formally start a company. I just started building Web sites. The Internet was just starting and people thought it was a big deal that I could do this, so I wound up making a nice little profit. That lasted a couple of years, and then I met a man named Robin Tator. Robin is a terrifically inventive and adventurous dude. He was working on an idea for a do-it-yourself site that would be called warehome.com. He started out asking me to lead the design of his Web site and wound up asking me to take over the entire development of it

The Internet bubble burst just when we were going to close the first round of venture capital funding. That was also about the time I was accepted to Princeton.

When I arrived on campus, I had only a few hours to settle in and negotiate with my new evangelical Christian roommate over who'd get the bottom bunk (I lost). The next thing I knew I was playing one of those corny camp name games with fifteen other bewildered freshmen and two overly enthusiastic juniors, in preparation for a weeklong canoe trip. The premise of this trip, known as Outdoor Action, or OA, was to ease us nervous and intimidated freshmen into the Princeton culture during the two weeks before classes began.

This was where I met Jon Beyer, a computer-science major from Maryland who seemed to me the only (other) sane guy on the trip. From the fun and games in the gym, we piled into a yellow school bus and headed out to the starting point for the trip, unsure what to expect. As we canoed down the Delaware River over the next seven days and stayed at trailer parks full of garbage, I started to miss Canada. Canada is a country full of nice people, clean air, and a sense of humility in the face of the awesome power of Mother Nature.

America is a big land full of people with big ideas, and unlike anywhere else I've been, it is full of people willing to take big risks on these big ideas. It is a land where failure is seen as a stepping-stone, not a tombstone. It is a land where truly anyone—even Hungarian-born Canadians like me—can live the American dream. But, as I discovered on my canoe ride down the Delaware, it is also a hugely polluted land, one where building a new housing development is more important than protecting the forest that stands in its way.

We returned to Princeton and the wonders of Frosh Week. I later figured out that the real point of this seven-day blowout was not to orient the incoming class, as they'd have you believe, but rather to give senior guys the opportunity to hook up with as many freshman girls as possible without any of them saying those dreaded three words: "I love you." For me, it was also a time when the myth of cheerleaders and football players that I'd seen in movies during high school came to life before my eyes.

Those first few weeks at school, you're bombarded by propaganda. Princeton has a million clubs and associations, and they all try to snag as many incoming students as they can. Out of the tornado of flyers, posters, and letters, one in particular caught my eye: an announcement of the Princeton Entrepreneurship Club's annual Business Plan Competition—Grand Prize $5,000. Second and third place were worth $3,000 and $2,000, respectively. I pointed this out to Jon and he was interested, too. This was big money for us. But we needed an idea. We played around with a bunch of nonstarting ideas, from selling photocopiers in bulk to cutting hair. Nothing that worked.

Pretty soon I was going to classes and staying up till four every night, trying to read the insane number of books assigned to me by each of my five professors. I took all kinds of classes—not economics but things like psychology and Buddhism. That October, a Princeton psychology professor, Daniel Kahneman, was the corecipient of the Nobel Prize for Economics—that's right, a psychology professor won the economics prize. Kahneman was looking at economics from a psychological point of view, such as asking questions about why and how people took risks or didn't. For instance, if you offer people the choice between receiving $100 this week or $110 next month, they are more likely to take the $100 right away. What he studied was being called "behavioral economics," and it really attracted me because it was all about thinking outside the box. I decided that I would create an independent major that combined psychology and economics.

Also that first semester, Jon and I grew to be good friends, despite how busy we were. I liked him from the start. He was shy and polite—the kind of guy who waits at the corner for the light to change instead of just jaywalking (I jaywalk)—and a fantastic computer programmer to boot. (He's also a total cycling nut and would eventually become captain of the Princeton cycling team.)

Though he isn't fundamentally an entrepreneur, Jon loves big ideas and has the passion and the problem-solving skills to make things happen. Before too long, Jon and I were enjoying the ever-escalating success of the "pre-street" parties we were throwing in my dorm room. By November, our modest get-togethers had grown from twenty people or so to more than one hundred students squeezing into our room. During our rapid growth we even had to open up the room of the girls next door to absorb the overflow of freshmen.

When our first official break came around at Thanksgiving, I decided to take three friends on a road trip to Canada, to show them what they'd been missing, living life in "da dirty South" (and to take advantage of the drinking age of eighteen). We took in a U2 show in Rhode Island and then piled into our little Ford Escort and drove directly up to Montreal, where we crashed in a run-down house that some Canadian friends—Jake Cohl, along with Steve Shaw and Pete McFarlane—had rented.

In high school, my friends and I had taken advantage of Canada's enlightened laws about the private cultivation of marijuana. That is to say, we were growing it. The most promising of these young seedlings was nicknamed Marley, and before I left for Princeton, it was decided that Marley, due to the "political climate" of the United States, would move to Montreal with my buddies and take up residence there in a dingy basement closet.

On the standard diet of chemicals, artificial light, and water, Marley hadn't been doing too well. Pete's reports on his condition had prepared me for the worst. Still, I was pretty anxious to see him. With an odd smile playing around his mouth, Pete led me to a closet at the bottom of the stairs. With a flourish, he threw open the door and cried, "Check him out!"

I could hardly believe my eyes.

Marley was . . . well, he was glorious. His leaves were fat and green, and his stalk was straight and thick. This was not the plant I'd said good-bye to a few short months earlier. "What happened?" I asked. "He was nearly dead!"

Pete was beaming. "I changed my approach, about four weeks ago."

"How?"

"Worm poop!"

I chuckled. "What?"

"I got a worm box and began feeding Marley worm poop," Pete explained. "He's been off the chemicals and on a steady path to recovery ever since."

"All thanks to worm poop?"

"Yup. It works like magic."

I thought about it for a second. "What the hell's a worm box?"

We went upstairs, where Pete, smiling like a proud father, showed off the secret to his success—an ordinary garbage can, no more than a couple of feet high, lined with black plastic. Inside were trays containing what looked like rich, dark soil along with watermelon rinds, eggshells, and other kitchen slop—and worms. Hundreds of them. Maybe even thousands. "They're red wigglers," he informed me. "And they've been doing very well. Super fast."

"I don't get it."

Pete sighed. "It's a home composting system. People have been using worm boxes for ages. I throw in leftover kitchen food and other scraps, like bits of newspaper, and the worms produce poop. It's the ideal fertilizer."

That moment, the proverbial lightbulb went off in my head, and it hasn't gone out since. We could take people's garbage (a service for which we could get paid), feed it to tons of worms (which is an environmentally chill process), get beautiful worm poop (which Pete had already proven was a fantastic fertilizer), and then sell it to the masses! The idea for TerraCycle was born.

We celebrated by inviting Marley's friend, Mary Jane, to the party. She gave us all a little kiss and we went to sleep, dreaming of poop and profits.

The epiphany in Montreal was serendipitous, since the Entrepreneurship Club's Business Plan Competition was right around the corner—the end of January, to be exact. Jon was as excited as I was, so we both jumped into exploring the business of worm poop with both feet.

First, we needed to show that we could make a profit, and one of the most attractive features of the idea was the cost of the raw materials. That is, there wasn't any. In fact, since our raw material was ordinary food garbage, people would even pay us to take it away—the cost of our raw materials was negative. That's a good thing.

So on the intake end, we were in the waste-management business, and we discovered early on that the market for waste management was *huge*! For example, in New Jersey landfills charge an average of $50 to take in a ton of garbage. On a national basis, Americans produce roughly 12–14 billion tons of waste each year, over 80 percent of which is organic. It is also this organic material, compressed in these landfills, that produces vast amounts of methane gas, which contributes both to ozone depletion and global warming. The big picture? Americans pay roughly $1 trillion every year to dispose of potentially harmful waste that might otherwise be fed to worms.

In other words, if someone could make something marketable out of worm poop, they could do the planet a favor *and* start with a negative raw material cost of over *$1 trillion*.

I didn't know a thing about writing a business plan, and neither did Jon, but we just decided to figure it out as we went along. To help us, and keep the party exciting, we enlisted eight of our closest friends and together began to write a business plan for what we called the "Worm Project." Our model revolved around making a tremendous amount of money by taking in a large volume of waste and feeding it to a huge army of worms. Once the worms had done their business, we would sell worm-poop fertilizer to farmers and landscapers.

The next step was to set out to see if there were any such businesses already in operation. Surprisingly, we found an entire worm-farming economy—and it was completely in a shambles, thanks to a lurid pyramid scheme led by Greg Bradley of B&B Worm Farms, a company he'd started only two years earlier.

Here's how it worked: B&B would host seminars in small towns, touting the wonders of worm farming. Bradley informed his audiences that red wigglers, the special worms used in vermicomposting, not only break down garbage at a ferocious rate but also double in population every ninety days. This was true enough. However, he went on to claim that he needed lots and lots of worms to fill lucrative contracts he had negotiated in Sierra Leone and with a large chicken farm in Ohio.

Armed with this story Bradley combed the country, looking for farmers who wanted to get rich quick and were willing to spend their savings to grow worms for him. The arrangement was simple. Farmers would invest roughly $30,000 for three thousand pounds of worms (roughly 3 million worms), as well as an additional $30,000 to build the worms a home. The worm population would double every ninety days, and Bradley guaranteed he'd buy back the increase in stock at the same $10 per-pound rate—to supply those large contracts around the world. Therefore, he explained to the farmers, they would be making roughly $10,000 a month happily farming worms.

Bradley offered a fistful of success stories: David White of Conway, Arkansas, who invested $5,000 and had seen a return of $87,569! Doug and Holly Stark of Peculiar, Missouri, had also invested $5,000 and saw a return of $82,610!

You can probably guess where this was headed. It eventually came to light that there were no large contracts with Sierra Leone (go figure), and the buyers who'd purchased David White's and Doug and Holly Stark's worms were not chicken farmers in Ohio but rather the next string of newly branded worm farmers whom Bradley had talked into starting a worm-growing business. This classic Ponzi scheme eventually netted Bradley more than $29 million from over twenty-nine hundred clients—clients who were left high and dry a few years later, when he died of a cocaine overdose in January 2003.

To this very day, there is tremendous speculation in the worm community over whether or not Bradley did in fact die, or whether he staged his own death and fled to an island somewhere in the Caribbean. We'll probably never know for sure. In one of life's little ironies, it turned out that Bradley "died" the same month TerraCycle would be incorporated.

Any possible competition from the worming world had been wiped out by the sour taste left behind by B&B, so there was no real competition from that direction. Other possible competitors were the landfills, but we planned on underpricing them because we would be making money on the other end. Besides, landfills were getting some pretty bad press, as people learned about their disastrous effects on the environment. Fresh Kills, the largest landfill in the world, was to be closed in a few months. Clearly, anyone would be welcomed who could come up with an alternative to landfills that could also turn a profit.

The only other competition could come from industrial composting sites, which take the home compost bin and magnify it thousands of times. Composting sites make a profit by taking in waste, just like our business model, and turning it into an eco-friendly finished product (compost) that can be sold to farmers and landscapers. The composting business model, therefore, was almost identical to the Worm Project's except for two key differences: the time it would take us to process the waste (ours was much faster), and the quality of the output (ours was much better).

Composting without worms takes between six and ten months, while worms can do the same thing in one to two months—*and* in a much smaller space (roughly a hundred times smaller). The largest industrial composter, in Edmonton, Alberta, is the size of seven football fields. Also, solid worm poop has a market price almost *one hundred times* that of compost. The best part? The vermicomposting process, as it's called, is virtually odorless, unlike composting.

As you can imagine, we were extremely excited.

We'd also discovered by this point that the way most people tried to compost with worms was in trays—just like Pete had in Montreal. The more garbage you had to dispose of, the more trays you needed. Even the most advanced ex-B&B worm farmers, whom we'd enlisted as advisors, used systems composed of hundreds of trays, which they were then forced to lift with forklifts in order to examine or tend. The less sophisticated ones, mind you, just threw a bunch of organic waste into a pile on the floor, then dumped the worms on top, waited two months, and then separated the wriggling masses from the resulting poop.

Since we were looking at converting entire landfills, this posed a serious logistical problem. Our biggest challenge, therefore, was to find a way to make and harvest worm poop on a huge scale both quickly and efficiently. Jon and I designed one system after another, but none of them seemed to be perfectly suited to our ambitious plan. The deadline of the business plan contest was getting closer, and if we didn't figure out this part of the business model, we'd be dead in the water.

As with many great (and not-so-great) ideas, the key to our solution came to me while I was sitting on the toilet, thinking about how horrible it is to be near one's own feces. I wondered: might worms feel the same way?

This called for some intense post-bathroom brainstorming. "I can't think of a single animal that likes hanging out near its own poop," I told Jon. "Not even in its general vicinity."

He agreed. "There's got to be a way to exploit that."

We pondered the possibilities for a while.

"What if we put the worms on a conveyor belt?"

"Keep going . . ."

"On one end of this conveyor belt, we'd place the organic waste, and the worms would slowly move toward it, eating everything in their path and leaving behind . . ."

"Poop! It would be like a poop-producing treadmill! We simply run the belt in the opposite direction that the worms are traveling, and their poop will just drop off the other end—loads and loads of it."

"Exactly!"

Two months later, our team had completed a one-hundred-page business plan that carefully laid out how the Worm Project would solve the world's landfill problems by converting billions of tons of organic waste per year into worm poop, all while making money on both ends. One late night in January 2002, we printed the ten copies of the business plan we needed to enter (running out of paper twice) and bound them. The only thing we didn't realize when we dropped them off was that we'd missed the deadline by one day.

There are more than two hundred business plan competitions in the United States every year, and they all follow the same basic outline: Teams are asked to submit their business plans, and if approved by a panel of venture capitalists (VCs) and successful entrepreneurs, they are invited to present in person for a strictly enforced fifteen minutes.

The Princeton Entrepreneurship Club forgave us being late and agreed to consider our plan. We waited. The judging wasn't completed until March, and by that time our team of eight had dwindled to three—Zack Faigen (one of my four roommates), Jon, and myself. The others just were not into the idea of a career in worm poop, we realized, and had enjoyed the novelty of thinking of starting a business more than actually doing it.

The first round of judging selected fifteen teams to present their ideas, which ranged from a student furniture exchange to a program that would allow students to instant-message questions to their teachers in class instead of raising their hands. Some of the concepts were impressive; others, not so much.

We had focused a tremendous amount of energy on our business plan, and sincerely believed we would win on its merits alone, so we hadn't thought much about the presentation. Everything was in that one-hundred-page proposal; all the judges had to do was read it. So we just winged the presentation. The wisdom of our view was confirmed when the first round concluded with the Worm Project chosen as one of the top four businesses to proceed to the final round.

We figured we had it in the bag.

In the end, we were the ones in the bag. To our surprise and dismay, it turned out that the judges had only skimmed our business plan and were impressed not by its contents but rather by the sheer weight of its paper and the incredibly small size of its type. They had advanced us to the final round on those merits alone. When the dust settled, we found that we'd come in fourth—the only finalist team to finish without prize money.

Jon, Zack, and I trudged wearily out into the cold winter air that evening, our heads hung low in shame. "I don't get it," I complained, "our business plan was well crafted and we considered every detail. Why didn't we win?"

The guys just shrugged and tried to cheer me up. Maybe they were right. Maybe I needed to think about something else for a change—anything but worms! I realized that, what with all the midterm exams and the competition, I'd hardly eaten in days. I suggested that we go out for a steak.

When my T-bone arrived at the table, the answer to my question hit me like a ton of "compost": we never had a chance of winning that contest! "Steak versus sizzle!" I cried out. "We just learned the difference between steak and sizzle!"

Jon and Zack looked up. "Huh?"

"Our plan was all steak, guys. A beautiful piece of steak, but just steak!"

"So?"

"So they didn't want steak," I explained. "They wanted sizzle. They wanted us to sell them on the plan."

Jon smiled. "I get it. The judges couldn't be bothered to read the plan because we did a crappy job explaining it to them."

"Sell the sizzle . . . ," Zack said, nodding. "It's all about the fifteen minutes. We've got to be able to go in there and tie everything up in a neat little package. Get people pumped and excited about it in fifteen minutes."

Jon agreed. "Because really, what's the use of a revolutionary idea like the Worm Project if we can't get it off the ground . . . if we can't convince people to buy it?"

Though we lost the Princeton business plan contest that cold day in March, we gained something more valuable: we understood the need for sizzle with the steak, a lesson we'd each carry with us for the rest of our careers. We'd figured out what we'd done wrong, but was it too little too late?

Life went on—reading, studying, partying—but I could not get the Worm Project out of my mind. No matter how hard

I tried, I just couldn't seem to get rid of it. I tried—I even spent some time painting posters for one of the university's drama clubs, but even then I couldn't forget about the Worm Project. I talked about it a bit with Robin, who loved wacky ideas and was completely into the prospect of selling poop for a living. Aside from our shared enthusiasm, however—and the two thousand worms living in my dorm room in a container about the size of a large shoebox—we didn't know how to make it a reality.

Luckily, Jon couldn't let the Worm Project go, either. Surfing the Internet, he came across an industrial-scale system for collecting worm-poop compost, Harry Windle's worm gin. The second I spoke to Harry, I could tell he was a complete nut, but he was our kind of nut—a crazy inventor, a mad-scientist type whose business was making massive worm machines and compost screeners. Harry's system hinged on the same conveyor-belt principle that our idea had, only he took the concept to a whole new level—literally. Harry's worm gin boasted conveyors stacked on multiple levels and could accomplish what we'd imagined in a tenth of the space.

All the excitement I'd felt when we began the Worm Project came flooding back. I quickly negotiated a deal with Harry: He agreed to build us a system that could handle Princeton's waste; he'd even do it for half price: a mere $20,000. Not that Jon or I had $20,000, or even $5,000, for that matter.

Armed with this renewed energy, Jon and I tackled the next step: Where would we get the waste for the worms to eat? Luckily the answer was all around us. We began lobbying Princeton to allow us to dispose of the school's dining-hall waste during the coming summer. We started with the head of the dining service. After five meetings, he gave his approval to the idea—we signed on to take the barrels of waste from Wilcox Dining Hall every day throughout the summer and bring them back empty by the evening.

But then we had to go to buildings management to get permission to have access to the waste over the summer. After five more meetings, they agreed. Then we had to go to grounds management to convince them to give us a place to put the worm gin. You guessed it—five more meetings. It took forever, but all the while we were honing our pitch—selling the sizzle to give the steak a chance.

At the thirteenth of the fifteen meetings, I couldn't wait anymore. School was almost over. I called Harry and gave him the go-ahead to start making the worm gin. By calling Harry and agreeing to buy a machine that I couldn't afford, we put ourselves on the line, but we believed in the Worm Project and were willing to do whatever it took to make it happen. We were about to learn that sometimes it takes more than you have to give.

With two weeks before the end of the term, we finally received official notification from the university. Jon and I combined our savings (amounting to $5,000) and sent that to Harry as a goodwill down payment. He said he would have it ready by the middle of June. Then I called an old buddy from high school, Anthony Green, who agreed to loan us $5,000 of his bar mitzvah money. In the same breath, I maxed out the credit cards my parents had given me and then called them to borrow the balance. Within a month, I'd accumulated the $20,000 we needed.

On a whim, and to make sure Harry was legit, I decided to drive down to Florida to visit him the weekend before school was out. I recruited Noemi Millman—a senior theater major who'd joined us a month earlier—to join me for the trip. We could only afford to rent the car for forty-eight hours, and it turned out that Noemi, like any typical New Yorker, didn't have her license, so I had to drive the twenty hours there myself.

On the way down, Noemi and I brainstormed company names. Some of the more notable ones we toyed with were Gia Green, Magic Worm, and TerraPoop. We finally settled on TerraCycle as we crossed over from Georgia into Florida. Before too long we arrived at Harry's, which lay in the middle of a swamp. Harry proudly introduced us to his cow, Betsy, whom he'd been employing as an environmentally friendly lawn mower. (The next time we were there, we ate Betsy for dinner.) We hung out for four hours, getting to know each other and talking about the gin, then hit the road again for the twenty-hour return trip. Somehow we made it home before the car was due back, though we had to bend the rules and let Noemi drive a little—a better option than me falling asleep behind the wheel!

Four weeks later, our new friend Harry showed up with our magnificent, brand-new worm gin, and twelve hours after that Noemi quit.

Jon quit his job in Maryland and ran to my rescue, helping to shovel the rotting waste of which we were now obligated to dispose. To celebrate, we threw a crazy launch party and invited all the Princeton people and the press. We had a terrific artist there, Rascal, who painted the composter while it was moving, as well as the artist and videographer Jim Budman, the brother of ROOTS cofounder Michael Budman. Everyone had a terrific time, drank too much beer, and stayed up too late, but it did land us some publicity in the local papers.

But mostly June was a dark month. In the whirlwind of buying the worm gin and convincing Princeton to let us do our thing, we hadn't calculated for the cost of food or lodging and found ourselves broke, sleeping on the floor of a friend's dorm room during the week, scrounging for meals wherever we could find them. In the morning, we would get up, pick up the morning's serving of waste, and take it down to the gin. Chipping and shoveling it into the rotary composter took until the middle of the afternoon. By about six we would have all that into the worm gin. Then we'd eat dinner and go to work on the business. We sent our business plan out to every venture capitalist firm we could find, in the hopes of securing some funding, and received nothing back but a steady stream of rejections.

As the summer wore on, things became increasingly bleak. The only relaxation for me was that I could spend weekends in Jim Budman's amazing studio in SoHo and explore New York. By the end of July, all we'd really accomplished was proving that the worm gin actually worked (phew!) and that we could indeed produce ample amounts of worm excrement. The rest of the plan, however, had been a total failure. We weren't being paid to take anyone's garbage away, and we hadn't sold a single pound of poop. There was no use in pretending anymore: the Worm Project just wasn't working.

I remember the night I finally realized this very clearly—lying on the floor, unable to sleep, and feeling my stomach turn as I planned what I'd say to everyone who'd loaned us the money to finance the worm gin. During a somber breakfast conversation with Jon the next morning, we decided to sell the worm gin on eBay and use the money to pay back some of our debts. I resigned myself to working at an investment bank over the next three summers in order to cover the rest.

As luck would have it, Jon and I had arranged to give a live interview about the Worm Project on a local AM talk-radio show that very morning. Instead of canceling, we decided it would be a cool way to wrap up our experiment in the worm-poop business before going back to school in September. So that clear morning in early August we rolled into the WCTC-AM studios near New Brunswick, New Jersey, in our trusty old pickup. Jon and I told our whole story to Bernard Springer, the talk-radio morning guy—from our first aha moment in Montreal to the business plan debacle, the woes of disposing of dining-hall refuse, and the bittersweet joy of producing some damn fine worm poop. The half-hour interview went by in a heartbeat, and we walked out with a tape of it in hand and a business to fold.

When we arrived back at Princeton, there was an e-mail

waiting in my in-box from someone named Suman Sinha. It was the kind of e-mail you almost automatically redirect to the trash. Good thing I didn't.

I clicked on it and rubbed my eyes.

It said: "I WANT TO INVEST. CALL ME." Six sweet words that would resurrect the Worm Project from the grave.

That night, Jon and I had dinner with Suman and his family at a local restaurant. He turned out to be a great guy—the sort of person who had an entrepreneurial spirit and a bit of money to play around with, and was just waiting for the right project to come along. He was attracted to the environmental advantages of the Worm Project and also thought he could make a little profit. After we ate, we drove down to the south end of campus to show him the worm gin. I explained exactly how it worked, then we stood there looking at it in silence for a while. Finally, Suman tapped me on the shoulder.

"So . . . how much do you need?"

"How much do you have?" My heart was pounding so loudly I could hardly hear myself think.

He smiled broadly. "How's two thousand dollars?"

"That would be great," I said without skipping a beat. "*Really* great."

"Glad to hear it," he said, then proceeded to write a check right on the spot.

CHAPTER 3

Hard Times

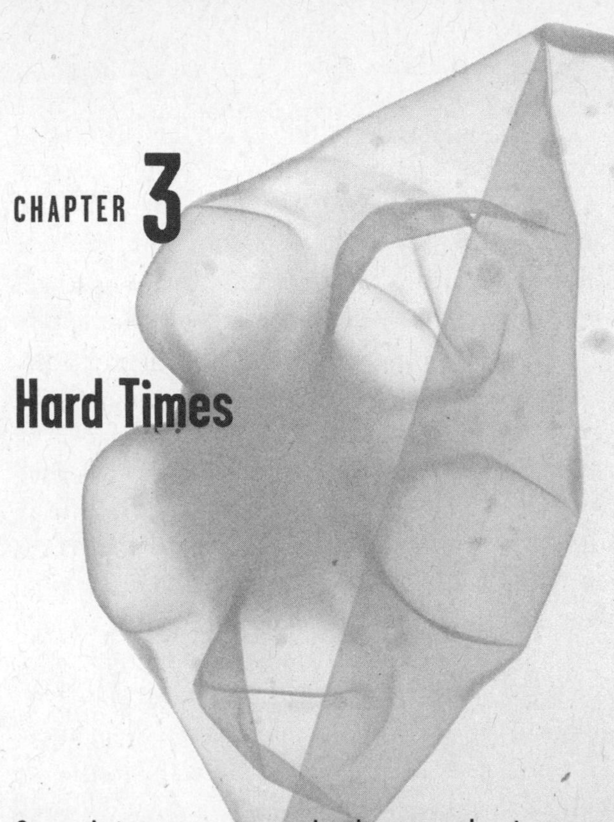

Suman's investment wasn't a bonanza, but it was enough to give us time to take a deep breath to regroup. Sort of, because soon we wouldn't exactly have a place to live. Our friend who had rented the dorm room over the summer was leaving for the last couple of weeks before school. So the morning after we cashed Suman's check, we headed over to a local real estate agent and began looking at anything we could have right away—apartment or office, it didn't matter.

Finally, we found a basement office on Nassau Street, Princeton's main street, right across from the university and about a half mile from the worm gin. There was one central room with two small offices on either side of it. The two offices became our bedrooms. Jon and I were still shoveling waste six hours a day, but we could shower in the gym and cook . . . well, who wanted to cook anyway? It had a small sink, so we could brush our teeth. And we knew that in another few weeks we'd be able to move into the dorm rooms we'd picked out at the end of freshman year.

The office wasn't completely raw space, but it needed some paint and, most of all, furniture. Office furniture was expensive, and besides, since we'd spent most of Suman's money on the rent and security deposit, we couldn't afford to buy anything. But we figured that somewhere on the Princeton campus, someone might be remodeling an office, and what would they do with the old furniture?

So the day after we took possession, Jon and I walked around campus. Sure enough, there was a pile of office furniture outside the offices of the campus business magazine, *Business Today*. We asked the people setting up the office what was going to happen to the furniture, and they said it was going to be thrown away. It was garbage, as far as they were concerned, and they didn't mind at all if we hauled it away. It was a natural—after all, we were in the waste-management business. Scrounging other people's rejects was our job.

So we brought around our Rent-A-Wreck truck and loaded it up with desks, chairs, lamps, file cabinets, whatever we thought we'd need—and could carry. The desks were old and metal and heavy, and we not only had to load them on the truck and unload them but carry them down a flight of steps and wrangle them into the office. But we acquired everything we needed, at a total cost of, well, $0.00.

Zero was a big number for us at the time. Our staff was zero, our customer base was zero, and our income was zero. Needless to say, our salaries were zero. When we had time and weren't exhausted, Jon and I looked for seed money, sending our business proposal out to every venture capitalist and investor we could find. The response was—you guessed it—zero. I called Robin Tator from time to time, asking him questions about how to do something or just for his ideas and his enthusiasm. He had a couple of companies he was running, a visual marketing business and an ice cream business, so summer was a busy time for him. But I knew from our experience together that he would be part of it when he could, and he helped as much as he could from Toronto during this time. We were still trying to build up the waste-management side of the business, but that was turning out to be a big zero as well. In order to make it really profitable, we would have to be processing hundreds and hundreds of tons of waste, which of course would mean dozens of employees and worm gins, not to mention millions of worms.

What we had lots of was worm poop—bags and bags of it sitting around the office. Thank God it didn't smell. In August, Princeton is a steam bath.

With a little regret and a whole lot of relief, we shut down the worm gin, boxed up all the worms, and stored them in the office. The worm gin was, after all, a hell of a lot of work and we had only contracted to handle the waste from the dining halls through the summer. But we had proved that it could generate compost magnificently—everyone who used our worm poop was amazed at how well it performed.

Then out of the blue there came a letter from a group named Tropika International, based in Toronto. Tropika was run by two men: John Litman, an enthusiastic, fortyish man; and a younger fellow named Daniel Pope, who handled the financial side of the business. Their pitch was that Tropika would find investors for TerraCycle so that I could build up the operations. That sounded great to me. This was the first time anyone other than Suman who wasn't a friend or a fellow student or a journalist had shown serious interest in TerraCycle. It was a kind of validation that I hadn't had before. They invited me to visit their office in Toronto so we could discuss terms face-to-face. I couldn't wait.

The first visit to Tropika was inspiring. It was a large office with new furniture, very well appointed in every respect. John seemed genuinely excited by the business and the prospect of growing it. He asked me how much money I was looking for, and I said around $20,000—thinking mainly that then I could pay off that credit card bill. We opened up a bank account and added John's name to it. We even put a little money in it.

They were even willing to lend us office space for Robin and Sam Ault, another Canadian, who had heard about the Worm Project at the Princeton business plan contest. At the time, he wanted to concentrate on finishing Princeton, but he invited me to dinner and said that he would like to work with us once he graduated in June. I had called him as soon as Suman had given us that first seed money and asked him to start working on the business plan. Now we really were international, with offices in Toronto and Princeton. I left that meeting very up, and eager to get working.

Obviously, however, we needed to bring in some money, so we brainstormed about what we could do. Probably the most successful gig we had was to bring in my friend from LA, Grant, to cut people's hair. There really wasn't any place that students could go to get a really good-looking haircut in Princeton. There were plenty of places for older people, but students went wild for a "celebrity hairstylist from LA, in for only one exclusive weekend." This was a real marketing coup actually. He was coming from Los Angeles, so we hyped it as a special weekend, limited-time-only opportunity and advertised all over campus. We got hundreds of girls and had Grant booked every thirty minutes all weekend. . . . What can I say, it paid the rent.

Most weekends that semester, we hosted an art party at the office. We found a unique formula that worked like a charm every time we did it. We would get a big piece of canvas, three feet high and eighteen feet long, and hang it on the wall of the office. We'd supply paint in cans on the floor, some beer and snacks and whatnot, and invite a bunch of our friends. We'd suggest to everyone that it would be great fun to fill up the canvas, however they wanted to, whether or not they'd ever done it before. Skill and talent, we emphasized, didn't matter here.

We'd start it off, or someone would, and gradually people

would start to have fun. Then an interesting thing happened. Once the canvas was filled, people would start painting each other. Pretty soon all their clothes would be filled. The next thing you knew all their clothes would be off . . . making their skin the canvas (wink). This happened every time! So we had discovered another reason to have art in the office, which we expressed in a simple formula that Jon and I wrote on the wall in pride: art + booze = naked people.

The parties had at least one positive business result, however. One of the regulars was a senior named Hilary Burt, who liked the whole TerraCycle vibe as much as the parties. She started helping out around the office for four or five hours a week. She was such a strong supporter of TerraCycle that she even convinced her father to invest $6,000 in us.

So with one thing and another, we managed to pay the rent for the first few months, but the beginning of school naturally created new problems as well as new opportunities. For one thing, Jon was a much more dedicated student than I, and when classes started, he made them his first priority. I should have been studying more, but the potential of TerraCycle was a more powerful motivator. I was still thrilled with the possibility of creating a huge business that would substantially reduce the amount of waste that was going into landfills. The whole concept had such beauty that I couldn't keep myself away from it. I wasn't the only one, either.

The New York Times had done a little article on us in the business section over the summer that called us "a Princeton success story." (The title was "The Employees Really Are Spineless"—everybody loved the worms.) There had been some other local articles and of course the radio program that had brought Suman in. We'd had inquiries literally from all over the world—Barbados, Hungary, Japan, and the United Arab Emirates. If nothing else, that kind of thing made me feel that we had a unique idea that could really fire people's imagination. *Inc.* magazine saw some of the publicity and assigned a reporter to talk to us.

Early in the fall, I asked Robin if he was willing to really put some time into TerraCycle, in return for a share of the business, of course. Now that the weather was cooling in Canada with the onset of fall, his ice cream business was going into hibernation, and he said he could split his time between his other projects and TerraCycle. He would come down every other week, sleep in the office, and help put the business on its feet.

Our biggest change was figuring out what business we were in. We took to heart one of the crucial lessons in entrepreneurship (not to mention life): when something isn't working, do something different. We hadn't found anybody outside the university who would pay us to haul away their organic waste, and it was pretty clear we weren't going to find anyone. What we had were bags and bags of the best fertilizer on earth.

Like garbage, fertilizer is one of those subjects that most people don't necessarily want to think about but is a fundamental part of our society and our economy. U.S. consumers spent a total of $37.7 billion on their lawns and gardens in 2001. Of that market, fertilizer and the various soils and mixtures for growing plants are estimated to account for over $6 billion and to be growing at a rate of 5 percent annually. Nearly 60 percent of Americans buy some kind of fertilizer or plant food every year. Even better, the organic part of the business was, and is, expanding at double the rate of the chemical side.

Worm poop has twice the calcium, three times the magnesium, five times the nitrogen, seven times the phosphorus, and eleven times the potassium of the surrounding soil. Nitrogen is a key ingredient in healthy plants—it promotes leaf growth and assists with protein synthesis and other vital plant functions. But even though it's crucial to growth, most plants are not able to extract nitrogen from any of the naturally occurring compounds that it usually forms unless it is also abundantly supplied with calcium. Worms not only provide extra nitrogen in their poop, they also have a calciferous gland that helps them process calcium. Moreover, worm poop adds busy microbes and bacteria to the dirt, which can be enormously important to the health of the soil. So it's not only feeding your plants, it's feeding your soil.

We had always imagined that we would sell the worm poop as fertilizer, but now we realized that we should focus on that. It was the product we had, and we had lots of it lying around. Let's sell it, we decided. That was a liberating moment in a way. Once we'd ditched the waste-management focus of the business, we could focus on selling worm poop: how to package it, how to market it, how to sell it. Our first attempts seem rather pathetic now: we just put the worm poop in bags that we had labeled "Pure Worm Poop." Black type on a white background. After all, we were a cutting-edge environmentally aware company—fancy packaging and lots of flash just weren't our style. We dressed in jeans and T-shirts and we carried our worm poop in plastic bags.

The idea was that the customer would simply scoop out the worm poop and spread it around in the garden, just as you would with a bag of planting soil or compost. I would put some bags in the back of my station wagon (which my parents had given me that summer) and drive around to local hardware stores and plant shops. I would walk into a store and the person behind the counter would say, "May I help you?" I would launch into my pitch about how I had a very unique product that I was hoping they would stock and so forth. Usually at that point they would cut me off and say that I would have to come back when the manager was there.

Eventually, I got smart and started calling before I visited a store, so that at least I would start out talking to someone who made the buying decisions. I would go through my spiel, and then I would pull out my bags of worm poop. Some people laughed in my face. The more polite ones would suggest that it would be hard to sell Real Worm Poop because the packaging didn't look very professional.

So it was pretty obvious that we needed to spend some time thinking about our packaging. Despite the fact that worm castings are not harmful and even, in some sense, quite clean, it was clear that people did not want to have much contact with it in its original state, fresh out of the worm. Robin, whose background is in marketing, came up with the idea of making it into a spray, which everyone thought would be more attractive to consumers and therefore the store buyers.

That tuned out to be a brilliant suggestion, because, not only was it more consumer friendly, but liquid fertilizer has a number of advantages over solid fertilizer. First, liquefying the castings makes them go a lot further (not that we had such a high demand at the time). Second, spraying it on the leaves of plants reduces the possibility of diseases attacking the foliage, increases the nutrients the plant can absorb (since the surface area is so much greater), and breaks down toxins more quickly. And on top of all that, some studies have shown that liquid fertilizer improves the nutritional qualities and taste of vegetables.

Of course, none of us knew anything about liquefying worm poop, so we went to the Internet. We found that worm-poop tea was a well-known subject among organic gardeners, and there were a variety of ways to produce it, at least on a small scale.

Making liquid worm poop is neither very difficult to do nor does it require expensive, complicated machinery. Basically, you take a plastic bucket and dump some worm poop in it. Then you put in a tube (or several tubes) attached to an air pump. Fill the bucket with water and start the pump so that there's a continuous and plentiful supply of air bubbling through the mixture. The point of the air is that disease-causing bacteria and such don't survive well in air. They thrive in anaerobic conditions, so as long as there's plenty of air going through the tea it is supersafe and beneficial for the plants.

After a day or so, you add sugar or molasses and pour the worm-poop tea you've just made through cheesecloth or a nylon stocking and you're ready to go. That is, you're ready to go . . . if you are a home gardener. If you're a business, like

TerraCycle, you're ready to put the tea in some sort of container that consumers can use—we had decided to put the tea in the eight-ounce plastic spray bottles that we'd bought, with a different label (though still my design) and a new name—TerraCycle Plant Food. Unfortunately, once you've put the tea in the bottle, there's no longer any air going through it. That means that harmful bacteria start growing in it. And most important, that means, if you're TerraCycle, you have to sell whatever you've bottled up in about twenty-four hours.

That was a problem, but at least now we had a product to sell.

In mid-October, the first *Inc.* magazine article hit the stands—it rocked. There was a big picture of me sitting in front of a pile of worm poop with some of the office graffiti art in the background. Then there was another big picture and an article about TerraCycle. Then most of another page was taken up with evaluations of the TerraCycle business plan by some venture capitalists and the editor of *Worm Digest*.

The overall impression was that TerraCycle was a big deal. Our long-term goal was formulated as "To become the dominant alternative waste-management company, with 30 to 100 worm gins functioning worldwide by 2010." And naturally we had offered our most enthusiastic expectations of how the business would grow—$2.5 million in sales in the next year, for instance. In other words, we'd said exactly what any ambitious entrepreneur would say. All in all, it was a fabulous boost. I didn't even mind that three out of the four judges gave us a failing rating. The important thing was that the article raised the profile of TerraCycle by an incalculable rate.

My hopes went through the roof when John Litman called around that time. I hadn't heard anything from him for months, though I knew from Sam that he and Daniel Pope had been helping out with the business plan. Now, all of a sudden, he had someone who wanted to invest. A Canadian who had moved to the Netherlands had put $40,000 into the business because he thought it was an unusual, interesting concept and the environment was going to be increasingly important. In fact, the money was already in our bank account. I was ecstatic. John asked me to come up to Toronto again to go over the offer and talk about how to structure the business.

Everything was going our way, so I was a bit mystified when Robin called up on Sunday and suggested that I take John's name off the bank account. When I asked him why, he just said that he thought it would be a good idea and that he'd tell me more when I arrived in Toronto. I didn't get there until late, but first thing Monday morning I went to the bank and did as Robin had suggested.

When John, Daniel, and I met, they started off by saying that since we now had other people's money in TerraCycle, we would have to structure the business a bit differently. Of course, I knew that we would have to give our investor a share of the business, but John suddenly seemed to be suggesting a great deal more than that. For one, he had decided on a person he wanted to bring in as CEO, someone with some "real business experience." Since I was only twenty and hadn't had any "real experience," that seemed reasonable in a way. However, we would have to pay this new person a substantial salary, and we didn't have any real income yet. Up to this point, after all, we hadn't yet paid anyone anything. I was just then hoping to be able to put Sam on at least a small salary.

That kind of thing went on for another day or two until it became clear, when I looked at all the numbers, that what was really going on was that Tropika was going to take the company away from us. Robin and I would have to give up most of our share of the company, and essentially any right to have any say in the direction or operation of TerraCycle. If it made a lot of money, of course we would do well, too—but it would no longer be our company in any real sense.

I went home and spent the evening talking to Robin and Sam. It was clear to me that I didn't want to give up the company, and Robin felt the same way. Sam, who had been working somewhat in isolation from us and right beside these guys, was a bit mystified that everything could go so sour so fast. We talked over some ways to work with John and come to a compromise that didn't involve us giving up TerraCycle, but he rejected them all. I had to bite the bullet.

The next day, I told John straight out that we just couldn't really go the way he was suggesting. He was furious, seething—I suspect he never imagined that we would just walk away from the deal. I left his office and went over to where I had been staying that week. Daniel Pope came around and tried to smooth things over, but I think he knew that the differences were so basic that there wasn't any way to go forward. We all tried to put the best face on a train wreck.

They didn't have to tell us that we weren't welcome anymore, but they did. Robin had only been in that office intermittently, and Sam cleared out the next day. When I got back to Princeton, I got a screaming phone call from John about the bank account. He went on and on about how I had no right to do that, and it was Tropika's money, and so on and so forth. Meanwhile we had called the investor and talked over the whole situation with him. He was very agreeable and let us keep the money. He didn't care about Tropika all that much, but he liked TerraCycle and what it represented. So we weren't entirely back where we started.

As a totally weird kind of compliment, within a few months Tropika actually reinvented itself as a worm-poop company. As CSRplus Vermicast Industries Inc., they currently provide both information and products to turn organic waste into worm castings. Their Web site even trumpets their association with us: "Our initial vermicasting venture involved refining and developing the business plan for TerraCycle—an early entrant into the large-scale production and retail distribution of worm castings 'tea' (a liquid organic fertilizer derived from the vermicasting process). Using advanced vermicasting technology, organic waste destined for landfills is converted to liquid plant food in just three weeks." Google them, they are still out there today.

Unbelievable.

It had been a crazy year—exhilarating, exhausting, confusing, disappointing, challenging, scary, and wonderful. I knew we had to get back to raising money as quickly as possible.

CHAPTER 4

The Carrot and the Stick

As if running a company that could barely cover next month's rent and that had a product with twenty-four hours of shelf life wasn't enough, I had to make a decision about Princeton. All that fall, I had tried to run TerraCycle and be a full-time student at the same time. It wasn't working. I wasn't even thinking about class when I was in class. Princeton didn't allow students to attend part time, so as the semester was coming to an end, I had to make a decision. I decided to drop out of Princeton.

Another person who provided a key link in those early days was Priscilla Hayes, the county solid-waste management person, who introduced us to the EcoComplex at Rutgers University. The EcoComplex is about as old as TerraCycle, having been started in April 2001 to "research and educate people about environmentally sound business practices." The Eco-Complex is located on the Bordentown Resource Recovery Complex (in other words: "the city landfill"—nice name, eh?). Since it was created to develop "innovative environmental technologies," TerraCycle fit in perfectly. For a while, in fact, we were about their only project (I guess other people didn't like the idea of working on a landfill as much as we did). At the EcoComplex, we could set up the worm gin again. We agreed that we would move in and we discovered that we were the only ones in the incubator.

Bill Gillum (the second person over twenty-five to join TerraCycle) took it on himself to get the worm gin up and running. Bill was a highly experienced chemist who had worked for Western Electric, AT&T, and Lucent but had decided to retire and find new challenges. We were certainly a new challenge, and we hired him to be what we called director of operations. That meant that he had to make sure things were running, so even with his Ph.D. from MIT and all that experience, he spent the first six months shoveling shit. We didn't really have any employees at that point. We were still depending mainly on interns for the grunt work, but Bill pitched right in.

Despite all the disappointments of not finding investors and of Tropika, we had been entering business contests and winning them. Our business model had been significantly refined, and we had jettisoned the waste-management side of the business. Even better than that, we had a terrific PowerPoint presentation. We had learned the value of the sizzle, and believe me our presentation sizzled. We entered the Princeton Entrepreneurship Club's business contest plan again, and this time we won the top prize. Unfortunately, now that we had an office and people we had to pay at least occasionally, as well as expenses, we kept on needing money. By the end of the month, even with the $5,000 from the Princeton contest and the other six business plan contests we won, our bank account was down to $500.

There was one glimmer of hope. The big gorilla of the

business plan contests was the Carrot Capital Business Plan Challenge. This was a nationwide contest sponsored by a venture capital firm named Carrot Capital, and the grand prize was $1 million in the form of investment capital from the company. Naturally, the competition rose with the size of the prize. In 2003, there were 750 entries in the contest. Everything was on the line with Carrot. It was do or die.

Having won seven other contests, we weren't entirely surprised that we made the first cut and had been named one of the twenty finalists, which meant that we would have to do our presentation in person in New York City. We stayed up the night before to get ready, refining the presentation, printing it out, and binding it on our Nassau Street office floor. Robin came down from Toronto and on April 26, 2003, a Saturday, we took our PowerPoint presentation into New York City one more time and did our thing at about two in the afternoon. We took a deep breath and did our pitch—a solid twenty minutes to three judges. We showed a bottle of TerraCycle Plant Food, though to call it our product was something of an embellishment. It was liquid worm poop in a new bottle.

The winners would be announced at a dinner that evening, so we hung out in the hotel for three hours until the dinner at the Forbes Building on Fifth Avenue. There was a cocktail party beforehand for Forbes's entrepreneur of the year—obviously not us.

I was wearing my usual casual outfit while everyone else was in the typical "investment banking getup"—suits, ties, the whole thing. Robin and I stood around trying to make conversation, but nobody was talking to us—it was sad. We were incredibly depressed at this point. Everyone was looking at us like we were dirt. At one point Robin nodded to me to go out of the room for a chat. He was thinking the same thing I was. "There's no point in staying here," he said morosely.

"We're out of it. We must be. Nobody's even looking at us. We might as well go home."

"There's one thing, though," Robin said.

"What's that?" I couldn't imagine what he was talking about.

"There's a free meal."

"Good point." I nodded. I was willing to cut my losses, but we might as well get everything out of it that we could.

So we went back in, and they called everyone into the dining hall. Robin and I sat down at our table, which turned out to be in the very back of the hall . . . to add insult to injury we were at the "boobie table."

There were the usual kinds of speeches, and the first course, and then they announced the ten teams that had not made it to the next round. Here it comes, I thought.

But no. They got to the end of the list and still hadn't said our name. Robin and I looked at each other with our eyebrows taking off. Those first ten didn't win any money, but everyone from this point on would get at least $100,000. That was a pretty good piece of change. So I spent the next course figuring out how many different ways we could use $100,000. After that course, they announced the next five. We were still in the running. After the next course, they would announce three more, all of whom would receive $250,000. That was when they served the entrée, which I just couldn't eat because I was so wound up. When they started announcing the next three, it was like the business plan contest version of Russian roulette, I was just desperately hoping not to hear our name.

And I didn't.

I didn't even bother trying to eat the dessert, whatever it was. I knew the next name I would hear would be the team that had won half a million dollars. I had no idea who the other finalist was—until their name was called first after dessert. We had won. Suddenly all those people who wouldn't talk to us were giving Robin and me a standing ovation as we walked up to receive the prize. It was surreal. Partly because there really wasn't a prize. At some later date, Carrot Capital would make us a formal offer of investment capital. At that point, I didn't mind. I took the bottle of wine they gave us, and after a little schmoozing, I went back home.

The next day was Sunday, so I called Bill Gillum to give him the good news and luxuriated in the thought that we wouldn't have to be spending so much time just raising cash. The only thing that bothered me was that David Geliebter, Carrot's managing partner, had mentioned something after the award about toning down the emphasis on the environmental benefits of our process. I didn't see the point in that, but I wasn't too worried about it then because there was so much else to talk about. Maybe we could afford an office with windows. Maybe we should have a manufacturing plant.

On Monday, the whole TerraCycle team—it must have been thirty people—went into New York City to open the NASDAQ, which was a really terrific moment. We were interviewed on CNBC's *Power Lunch* and a couple of other news shows. We were generally feeling pretty terrific about things. I talked with David Geliebter about him coming to see the office and the worm gin at the EcoComplex. He agreed that was a good idea, because Carrot would work up a deal sheet about the specifics of the offer and how it would be paid, and so forth. The prize, it turned out, was really just a term sheet—an offer of funding from Carrot.

That next week, Geliebter and some others came down and looked over everything. At one point, they took me aside and started to talk about their plans for TerraCycle. As he'd suggested at the dinner, they really weren't too interested in the environmental benefits of producing and selling worm poop. They did see a big opportunity in the organic nature of our product. They must have figured that organic fertilizers and plant food would be a fast-growing market for consumers, which is what we figured, too.

Then the next week, they brought me into New York and talked some more about how they wanted the company to develop. They would bring in their own team to take over everything about the business—manufacturing, production, sales, marketing. They would make me the public face of the company, but it would just be a company that sold an organic fertilizer. They told me I would become famous, and rich, and I wouldn't even have to work that hard at it. In other words, they wanted to take over the company, too, even though I would still be a part of it. I said then that I didn't think that was necessarily the best way to go forward and went back home to Princeton to think things over.

Eventually they sent me an e-mail that laid out essentially what they were going to offer. It boiled down to two major items: lose the environmental side of the business, and lose the entire current staff. Not only did I think that was unfair to the people who had been so generous with their time and effort, but it didn't make any sense to me. The garbage-based business model was what made TerraCycle distinctive and had attracted so much attention and support.

I called Geliebter and ended up saying, "If that's the way the things are going, I don't think we'll be able to come to terms." He wasn't too happy, but at that moment he just hemmed and hawed. Later that week he sent a five-page letter about what a terrible decision I'd made and how disappointed he was and how with Carrot, TerraCycle could be everything and without Carrot Capital, it would be nothing. I didn't respond to it, and I heard nothing more from him, so in fact Carrot never really made us the offer that was the prize we had won. I think he was just shocked that anyone would turn down the money. By that time, I was becoming an expert at it.

I was also becoming an expert at living on the brink. After all was said and done, we still had only $500 in the bank. There weren't any more business plan contests to enter, at least for that year. We could try making money the old-fashioned way—by selling a product and getting paid for it, but we still didn't have a way of putting vermicompost tea into production or delivering it to stores or the consumer in any form that would be attractive. We had to think of something fast.

So the day after we turned down Carrot's proposals, we all met in the basement office on Nassau Street and tried to figure out what the hell to do next. It was a moment of desperation. Robin dropped into an office chair with a weak spring and nearly flipped over. He glared at me.

"It's garbage, dude, you have to watch out for that one," was all I could say. We were all agreed that Robin's idea of vermicompost tea was the most consumer-friendly way to deliver the fertilizer. Bill was going to work on stabilizing the tea so that we could assure stores that it would last on the shelf. We knew that it wouldn't go "bad," but what we didn't know was how much of its nutrients would remain effective.

But how were we going to get the bottles we needed to hold the tea to take to the stores to bring in the cash? We had everyone in the meeting, including our advisors—it was a Hail Mary moment. If we didn't come up with a solution we were finished. I asked Robin how many bottles we could buy for, say, $200.

"None," he said. "They won't let you buy anything unless you buy in bulk. The minimum order is something like a thousand dollars. More, probably."

Robin tossed in an epiphany: "Why not temporarily grab used bottles from people's recycling?"

A light went off in my head. "Wait, that's a brilliant idea." They all looked at me. "We have a product that is made from garbage. In fact, the product itself would be considered garbage by some people. Why not package it in garbage?"

"Well, it's garbage, for one thing," Bill said sarcastically.

"Look at the furniture you're sitting on," I said. "We picked it up out of what was essentially the garbage pile. It works perfectly well." Robin pointed at his chair. "Well, mostly perfectly well."

"How are you going to get them?"

"We'll pick them out of recycling containers."

"We're just going to be filling them up with liquefied worm poop, after all," Robin pointed out.

"Look, this is just a temporary solution until we can afford to start buying new bottles again. We'll stick on a label and start selling them tomorrow," I said.

"You're going out tonight?" Bill looked dubious.

"We need the money. You gonna join us?"

After the meeting broke up, I got some extra-large garbage bags and gathered together four of the interns. Out we went to look through recycling bins for any kind of plastic bottle that wasn't crushed. I figured that we'd just recycle again the ones that were an odd size. Although I didn't expect to be doing this for the rest of my life, I really liked the idea that, as with the worm poop, we were turning something that people thought of as waste into something useful.

For those of you who don't know the town, Princeton is one of the more upscale places you would ever want to live in. Naturally the residents are good about recycling, so nearly everybody had a recycling container. It hadn't occurred to me that anyone would object to us going through garbage cans and sorting out the plastic bottles, but after we'd been collecting bottles for a couple of hours, suddenly we heard police sirens, and a couple of patrol cars pulled up, lights flashing. Several Princeton cops slowly pulled themselves out of the cars, waving their flashlights in our eyes. "What do you think you're doing?" one of them demanded.

I couldn't help but remember Wilcox Hall's food waste and the campus police wondering if we were stealing garbage. I tried to explain what we were doing and why, but the police couldn't understand that we just wanted to collect bottles and reuse them for our business. They were not happy, to the point where it actually became a little hairy. "We'll let you go this time," they said, "but if we catch you doing this again, we'll have to lock you up. It's against the law to go through people's garbage." At least they let us keep all the bottles.

We went back to the office. The other interns were coming in with their collections, so we dumped them all out on the floor and started sorting. Between the five of us, we had assembled a pretty substantial number of bottles. I expected that we would have all different sizes and shapes, so I was very surprised to see that there were only four sizes of bottles: two liter, one liter, half a liter, and twenty ounces. But what was an even bigger surprise was that for any given quantity, the heights, the bases, and the thread of the cap were all identical. The only real difference between them was the contour of the bottle.

That may not seem like something that could provoke an epiphany, but it did for me. What's important about the similarity of the bottles is that they could be run through high-speed bottling lines. And that meant that TerraCycle Plant Food could be mass-produced. Sure, at that moment, we were going to pour vermicompost tea into the bottles using jugs and funnels, but in the future we would be able to run the bottles through a bottling line and crank out thousands and thousands of bottles of plant food. What we had seen two hours ago as a temporary stopgap solution suddenly became the solution.

At that moment TerraCycle Plant Food was born. It was a huge turning point, and it all happened because we had turned down the Carrot Capital money. That forced us to try to find value in something that wouldn't cost us anything (which is somewhat like what the worms were doing for us)—that is, find value in something that had negative value for everyone else. Because we turned down the money we became the first product in the world (and still are today) that is made entirely from and packaged entirely in waste!

The idea of finding value in what people are willing to pay to get rid of is one of the fundamental backbones of eco-capitalism, as I think of it now. Think of it this way: There are two major components in a used bottle, the plastic and the shape. In the recycling model, the plastic has positive value, because it can be sold as a commodity. But in order to do that, you destroy the shape and reduce the plastic to a form that is useful for making something new. So the shape has, in a sense, negative value. All this takes time and energy, which is the reason why people argue back and forth about whether it's really an environmental plus to recycle bottles. Not only is energy expended in transforming a soda bottle into a usable material, there's also the cost of the trucks and the diesel fuel they burn and so forth.

However, if you can find value in the shape of the bottle, as we had, you're not only finding value where other people see waste, you're also saving the time, money, and energy needed to make use of the value of the plastic. To put it simply, reusing something is inherently more profitable that recycling something (and better for the environment).

This is a basic paradigm of eco-capitalism—that an object can have components that are waste and components that are valuable. The idea is to focus on what is "waste" and find a way to use it—for us that was to take advantage of the shape rather than treat it as a negative. Almost every time you buy something these days, you're almost inevitably buying an array of goods. Suppose this book is giving you a headache and you need to buy a bottle of aspirin. In addition to the hundred tablets of aspirin you buy, you're also buying a piece of cardboard that packages it, the plastic it's wrapped in, the bottle that holds the tablets, sometimes a little piece of cotton, for a reason no one can remember, and the luxury of having it shipped from the factory where it was produced. You're probably also being awarded a free plastic bag as a bonus. You may not be able to think of a way to use each of these items, but you probably can find a use for some of them. When you do, you're unlocking the power of waste.

It turns out that every year, Americans discard (not

recycle—just throw away) more than 200 *billion* soda bottles. The amount of waste is astounding, and the impact on the environment truly staggering. Currently, it takes about 63 million gallons of oil per year to manufacture disposable water bottles for the United States alone. While that may be a drop in the bucket, when we're done drinking our water, over 85 percent of those bottles wind up in landfills (where they take up to a thousand years to degrade) and incinerators. When they're burned, they release a variety of poisons into the air.

However, there's even a further problem. Between 1995 and 1998, the kind of plastic used in these bottles (polyethylene, usually called PET) increased by more than 50 percent—mostly because of the introduction of the twenty-ounce soda bottle. At the same time, recycling of this type of plastic *declined* nationally, from about 40 percent in 1995 to 25 percent in 1998. The problem for recyclers is that these containers are both bulky and lightweight—they take up a lot of room in the truck but they still don't weigh very much. And weight is the way recyclers get paid. "If you have a truckload of plastic, you're still not carrying much," says Rosalie Green, an Environmental Protection Agency (EPA) recycling specialist.

To complicate matters, plastic containers can be made from several different kinds of resins, and each kind must be sorted separately before it can be recycled—a costly endeavor. Plus, the amount of energy saved using recycled materials instead of virgin resin often is minimal, so companies have no inducement to use such materials. "If there is no incentive for manufacturers to make products that are sustainable, we're not going to have sustainable material use," says Bill Sheehan of the Atlanta-based GrassRoots Recycling Network. "The way the system is set up now, we taxpayers have to pay whatever it takes to handle what manufacturers throw our way in terms of packaging."

That night, of course, we were focused on more immediate problems. We took the bottles, cut off the labels, rinsed them out, and using our trusty funnel filled them with liquid worm poop and slapped on a sticker we had recently printed on the ink-jet printer in our office. The next morning we started going to small retailers in our area. One of the interns at the time, Ryan Salcido, sold the first ten cases out of my station wagon. We were on our way and starting to make sales!

CHAPTER 5

The Big-Box Approach

Once we had the concept of making everything about TerraCycle Plant Food from waste, the floodgates opened. The next thing was to figure out where to get the spray trigger tops. That wasn't something people were recycling in their garbage in any large numbers, so we would have to go elsewhere. Robin began talking to remainder companies—companies that deal in what other companies no longer want. And he discovered that there was an enormous waste stream out there of—among many other things—trigger spray tops. This happens when a large consumer product company decides to change the packaging for its window cleaner, for example (though you could substitute any product that uses a spray top)—they want their trigger tops to be blue instead of white, or streamlined instead of boxy, or whatever.

Once their new design is ready to go, they don't wait until they've used up all the old spray tops, and not uncommonly they will simply throw out one million or half a million pieces.

The company doesn't want to take up warehouse space with items they'll never use, so they can either pay a waste removal company to haul the stuff away or the remainder companies will pick it up and pay a few pennies a ton for them, so it's good for the company.

In fact, when we could afford to buy new bottles, they turned out to be more expensive than the used ones. All this was the foundation of our eco-capitalist strategy. Up to this point we had a company that was environmentally friendly, but like most companies, it was based on making a profit. With the concept of the waste stream being redefined as a resource stream, we moved a step beyond being environmentally friendly capitalists. We were now able to make a profit by taking things out of that waste stream, with the by-product of improving the environment. It broke the traditional paradigm of eco-business. Today the cheapest way to make a bottle is to use virgin plastic; if you want to go more environmentally friendly you may consider adding recycled content (which will raise your price). If you want to go super eco-friendly you may consider corn-based biodegradable plastic, but with that choice your cost will go up again. Today's paradigm is simple. The more eco-friendly you want to be the more it will cost you and in turn your customers. However, if you use a used bottle you are only paying for the plastic (not the shape), and by definition it will always be the cheapest choice. And without question, reusing a bottle is way cheaper and more eco-friendly than making one (no mater what you make it from). In the end, we had fused profit making with environmental consciousness. We were making cash from trash.

Waste is an entirely human concept. There really is no such thing in nature as waste. Everything is used; everything decomposes to become the building blocks of something else. More than that, the concept of waste is entirely a modern human idea. Basically, it didn't exist until the twentieth century with the invention of plastic and complex petrochemical materials. Until the middle of the twentieth century, most people, even those in economically developed nations, couldn't afford to discard clothes or furniture until they were worn out. Even if they threw out their shirt or chair, since these items were made from plants, they would decompose in a matter of years. It was the invention of complex materials (such as plastic or Styrofoam), materials that aren't natural food to another organism, that created the idea of waste.

During this time I was driving around New Jersey, visiting local retailers selling the worm poop, and for the first time we started to see some steady, if very tiny, income. In addition, we were constantly giving away free samples to get people to try the product. Which meant that we needed a steady supply of bottles. Since raiding Princeton's recycling bins was not an option, Robin and Bill began investigating the large-scale recyclers, but very often their bottles had been crushed and couldn't be salvaged. Eventually, we would find dependable sources of high-quality used bottles, but that was still years in the future. We still didn't have the money to buy bottles. We needed a new idea to get the waste bottles.

It came to me one day that there was an entirely different way to get quality used bottles: ask people to collect them. After all, so far we had survived in large part on the volunteer help of interns. People were willing to work for free when they felt they were doing some good or learning something valuable. That is, they were making a profit, just not a cash one. And since I was still very much oriented toward school as a way of life, I had the idea of using the local schools to help us collect bottles. We would go to the local schools, do an assembly about recycling and reuse, and ask the kids to collect bottles for us. We'd give them a giant box and every morning they could bring in their quality used bottles and throw them in the box.

That didn't seem to me enough of a profit for them, or for the school, which would be giving us the space for the box.

Sure, they were rescuing all those bottles from the incinerator or landfill, but I thought that they deserved something a little more tangible. Why not make it a fund-raiser for the school? We would pay the schools a very small fee for each bottle they collected, and of course we'd pick up the bottles.

Strangely enough, TerraCycle had unknowingly reproduced the old printing business model of the nineteenth century. Like the paper mills of that time, we needed a product that was not readily available from commercial sources—in large part because we were looking for something that had been used already. Same thing with the paper mills. In the nineteenth century, printing was almost entirely a barter economy. There were few industrial sources for rags and scraps, so ragmen became key players in the paper business. Ragmen, who often collected much more than rags, would in turn sell what they collected. In the case of rags, they would go to the paper mills to make rag paper. In fact, rags could be substituted for money. Households paid with rags for what they bought from peddlers and stores, who sold the rags to paper mills.

In the next step, clever businessmen (they were not yet called entrepreneurs) tried to make it worthwhile for housewives to give up their rags and scraps of cloth. They established systems for collecting rags from households and conveying them to the mills, and they propagandized households relentlessly in an effort to get them to collect rags.

Of course I knew none of this at the time, and it didn't matter. We first tried out the idea not at a school, since it was the end of the school year, but at a church not too far away from Princeton. The pastor there was very interested in TerraCycle, but he was still a little skeptical, especially when it came to asking his young parishioners to collect bottles. But finally I convinced him to let us try, and so one morning I stood up in front of about fifteen ten-year-olds. I had brought everything I could think of to sell the idea. We had a television with a VCR to show a video about TerraCycle, and we brought some worms and some of the garbage that we fed them. We brought in the big box for the church lobby. I evangelized for fifteen or twenty minutes about recycling and reuse and how they could make the earth a better place by giving TerraCycle their old soda bottles.

When I was done, I asked if they had any questions. One little boy raised his hand. "How does a worm poop?" I have to say I hadn't prepared for that particular question. It was all about the worms for them. They loved touching them; they asked about what they ate, how long they lived, and how big they got.

Whether it was the worms or the environment, the bottle brigade program was a terrific success. The kids were excited by the idea of TerraCycle, but maybe even more they were excited at the idea that they could go into a store and see a bottle that they personally had collected. I don't know that anyone ever would have that experience, but it was possible, and I think that gave them some of the motivation to collect the bottles. After all, the more they collected, the more likely it was that they would see their own bottle on the shelf one day. Meanwhile, they were also earning money that their school or church could use for something. It was a win for everybody involved.

By the next school year, the program began to take on a life of its own. After all, it was an assured way of raising money—there were plenty of bottles around and nobody was going to do anything with them. By the end of that year, there were thirty groups regularly collecting bottles for us.

Meanwhile, the disaster with Carrot Capital turned out to be a huge bonus for us. Though we had turned the money down, we hadn't lost the sizzle. Carrot's interest was a signal to others that there was something real here, and I was able to bring in some small investors that kept us going. Then in May or so, as a favor for one of these small investors, I went to the annual meeting of a company named Universal Display, which had nothing to do with TerraCycle and sounded like something from a science fiction story. But that's the sort of thing that happens when you're trying every possible way to get financing for a start-up.

When the day came, it was the last thing I wanted to do. I got lost on the way and almost went back home in disgust. But I stuck it out and finally found the place. So I walked into this meeting room and took a seat while Universal Display was presenting its goals for the next year. It wasn't really the most exciting presentation I'd ever seen, which is maybe why the person next to me started to chat. He asked me why I was there, and I said, "Oh, I'm really just doing a favor for a friend. This really doesn't have much to do with my business."

"Well, that's very nice of you. My name's Martin Stein. What's your business?" The funny thing was that he seemed really interested. It made me think of Suman Sinha a little. So I told him that I was starting a company that used worms to make fertilizer, and he kept asking questions, and after about ten minutes, he shook my hand and asked, "How much money do you need?"

I was tired and wasn't up to figuring out how much Martin was really likely to invest, so I just said, "Five hundred thousand dollars." Why not, I figured, he'd probably laugh.

But he just said, "Okay, I'm in. I'm your partner." We shook hands, and he said he'd call me the next day and visit. I was still pretty skeptical. I wasn't even completely sure that he understood what the business was all about, so it seemed pretty unlikely that he would actually participate.

But he called the next day and came down to see the business—that is, the office where I slept and worked. Bill gave him a tour of the setup at the EcoComplex, and evidently he asked Bill if I would be a good investment. I don't know exactly what Bill said, but the next day the money was wired to my bank account! Which just goes to show that you should never dismiss any opportunity, no matter how unlikely it seems on the surface. Over the next year, Martin was always ready to help. When I called him up, he would say, "How are things going? How much money do you need?" More than that, he became part of the company family.

Meanwhile Bill Gillum, when he wasn't making the compost and making the compost tea and fulfilling the orders, started a huge test to determine how effective TerraCycle Plant Food was.

There was a funny thing about the EcoComplex: since it was government run we always had chain gangs come through and help clean up the place. Robin, being a smoker (shame on him), realized that since inmates couldn't smoke we could get a whole day's labor with a simple promise of a single cigarette. Since Bill needed more people, we promised one of the inmates, Ron, a full-time job when he got out of the can. Ron came onto the scene just when Bill needed him the most. He even slept beside the worm gin.

For the experiment, Bill kept records on six hundred plants, vegetables, and flowers, each of which had to be precisely watered and measured every day for the entire summer. Then they all had to be pulled up to measure the root growth and a dozen other things that would show that TerraCycle Plant Food was actually an effective way of stimulating plants. It was a complete success. At the same time, he had to keep the worm gin going and keep it supplied with organic waste, which we bought from various places around the state. What made that difficult was that you couldn't be sure that the garbage would be the same all the time, and since the worms can only process what they're given, Bill also had to find ways to make sure that TerraCycle Plant Food actually contained what the label said it contained.

Bill and his team concluded that our worm poop was actually on par with other commercial plant fertilizers. That is, not only did it increase root growth and protect against disease, it also had amounts of nitrogen, phosphorous, and potassium that would make it comparable to other consumer fertilizers on the market.

It was at the end of this experiment that Ron disappeared. Turns out he stole a single shoe from a store near the Eco-Complex. After serving his time for the great shoe heist, Ron is now a greater at a local Wal-Mart.

Up to this point we had followed the advice of just about everyone we talked to in regard to how to build your brand in stores: "You go to the little stores and build your brand up, and then you go to a bigger store and a bigger store, and finally, when you've really established yourself, you might go to a major big-box retailer." Oh, and if you went to Wal-Mart they'd destroy your price and kill you, 'cause that's what Wal-Mart likes to do—they eat little suppliers for breakfast!

So we began with the "start-small" model and it was a pain in the ass. The local stores would buy a case here and a case there. Then we'd have to ship them cases individually, invoice individually, get them to pay us, and deal with any problems that arose individually. What was really annoying was that we never really had any idea if the product was selling. They might reorder when they sold out, or then again they might not. Moreover, to even be given the opportunity to sell to a small retailer you have to go through a distributor like ACE Hardware that will take 5 percent to put you in their catalog, 10 percent for this and 2 percent for that—oh, another 3.5 percent for the thing they forgot to mention. The whole system is a hindrance to big growth.

We weren't growing fast enough, and that's an understatement. We were barely bringing in $1,000 per month. We had to drive and pick up the soda bottles in my station wagon; turns out it could hold exactly 854 bottles. Clean, fill, and label the bottles manually. It was incredibly labor-intensive—every aspect of it. After a year we had about thirty organizations collecting bottles for us, providing us just enough bottles for these little orders. Without Martin, we never would have made it.

The only good thing that happened to me during this time

began in the office of one of our investors, Victor Elmaleh, the man best known for bringing the original Volkswagen bug into this country. I was sitting in Victor's office with another TerraCycle person, talking with Victor and one of his staff, when a girl walked in, looking surprised to see us there.

Her name was Soyeon Lee (although I think she purposely never introduced herself to me). Turned out she was a concert pianist studying at Juilliard and had just won Juilliard's William Petschek Piano Debut Award, the highest honor for a pianist at that school, that included presenting a concert at Alice Tully Hall. Victor had evidently decided to do some matchmaking, so he invited her for lunch on the same day that I was in his office to discuss his investment.

Soyeon thought she was coming in to talk about her concert and was rather dismayed to walk into a roomful of guys. She definitely hadn't come there to be set up. Even though Victor insisted that we sit next to each other, she showed very little interest in having a conversation with me and didn't hide it. Her career was taking off at that point, and she surely didn't seem too excited about being set up with a dropout running a fledgling worm-poop business.

Victor was not put off. When the lunch was over, he volunteered to have his car drive Soyeon back to the Upper West Side, and then also suggested that the driver drop me off at Penn Station. Amazingly, that ten-block ride took forty-five minutes (the driver may have gotten some further instructions from Victor to take his time), so we had a lot of time to get to know each other. The first ten minutes or so were pretty awkward, but things improved from there. I asked a few questions just to chat a bit, and while remaining cordial, she pretty much responded with a word or two. Finally, nearing Penn Station, I offered her my business card, which was made out of upcycled blue jeans, and she took it and said that she didn't have a business card to exchange. "Would you like it if I made you some business cards?" I asked. She said that would be all right.

I spent the next few nights making each card by hand and

called my friends to ask for advice on how to approach someone that I felt was clearly out of my league.

A week later, I went to her concert in New York City, which was the first time I had been to a solo piano recital. I was incredibly intimidated, especially after the concert, when she was swarmed by hundreds of people. After everyone left I gave her a pack of business cards. That broke the ice, she invited me to come out with her friends for drinks, and we married in May 2008.

Meanwhile, TerraCycle needed something to boost business. The model clearly wasn't working, so we tried a bigger situation—the trade shows. You'd have to sit in these places—these huge convention centers—and guys would walk up and down the aisle and you'd have to pitch each and every one of them that walked by your booth, and in the end they might order a case. "That's cute," they'd say. "Maybe next year. Could you give us a free case and we'll see if it sells and if it does maybe we'll buy more?" It was brutal. I hated every second of it. I wanted dot-com growth rates, but we were growing like a nice little organic consumer-products company—slow and steady, hoping for word of mouth or guerrilla publicity or lightning to jump-start sales.

The shows didn't build up the business and we always spent more money traveling—San Francisco, Houston, Chicago—and setting up for the shows than we ever made. I remember in particular a show in Las Vegas that was on two floors and we were in the basement. We had spent $15,000 on the booth and the travel. It was three days long, and in that whole time two people passed us. I wound up sleeping on the floor for half the show. Robin was there with me, and one time I woke up and looked at him and said that this was the most screwed-up way to do this. We were going to stop. We were going to go to the biggest stores and beat down their doors with a battering ram.

Big-box retailing came onto the scene in the 1950s and today those stores are by far the leaders in each industry. In other words, today, if you sell to Lowe's, Wal-Mart, and Home Depot, you will reach over 75 percent of the entire lawn and garden market in America. Or if you sell drain cleaner to Home Depot (as we do now), you're selling to 25 percent of the entire drain cleaner market.

So naturally, flying in the face of all odds, Robin and I started to call the big-box stores—Wal-Mart, Home Depot, Lowe's, all of them. It was really hard to get through. Nobody picked up. So we kept calling—every hour on the hour. We even changed what phone we called from and only left one message a day. After thirty-five days, a buyer at Home Depot finally picked up the phone and gave us thirty seconds to make our pitch. I told him that we have "the world's most eco-friendly product, its made from and packaged in waste, and best of all its cheaper than the competition." Then he said that it sounded interesting but we should talk to so-and-so in a different department. So-and-so passed us off to someone else, and someone else passed us off, but finally we were passed to the dot-com person, who gave us a meeting.

We were ecstatic. This was going to be the big test for us. If we made it, we might be able to establish a new business model for the company and leave behind the whole outmoded system that, as far as I could tell, was going to choke us off before we even had a chance to establish ourselves.

Of course this was dot-com, so it was really for peanuts, but we went crazy with it anyway—we brought worms and plants grown with and without the fertilizer; we had the PowerPoint presentation; we wouldn't let them say no. They ended up making an order, maybe because it was easier to do that than turn us down. They weren't risking very much. But it was our first big order, a pallet of product. So we flew back from Atlanta and went directly to the EcoComplex to help Bill fulfill the order.

The bottling line, at this point, was still fairly primitive (plastic funnels). We had a dishwasher to clean out the bottles. When they were dry we labeled them with a contraption made of four paint strippers. These are things that basically look like hair dryers but deliver a lot more heat. We had bought a bunch of what are called shrink-sleeve labels. You would slide a label onto a bottle and lower it into the middle of these four paint strippers, which were arranged like the points of a compass, but pointing upward. You had to wear a glove or you'd burn your hand, but the hot air would shrink the label securely onto the bottle. Perfect, if you did it right. Then we'd screw on a top, and box them. The boxes, of course, were overruns. I remember we had a lot of Dasani boxes at one point. Of course we had to break down the boxes and turn them inside out so that the Dasani label wasn't showing. Then we'd stamp them with a rubber TerraCycle stamp and bang, there you were.

In the end, we shipped as much in that one order as we had shipped in the previous six months. All while we were still calling Martin Stein for additional investment on a regular basis.

Robin and I both felt that this was a much better opportunity for us than the small retailers. While we certainly weren't going to ignore them, we could grow in both directions. Since we were already priced less than the larger companies for a comparable size bottle of plant food, the large retailers didn't need to begin by driving our price down.

This is another fundamental of eco-capitalism: unless you make the product equally economical for consumers, they aren't going to buy a product they don't know anything about. Sure, some products that are "organic" or "environmentally friendly" have gained a certain cachet that allows them to build their brand at a higher price point, but that's only true for a niche market—if you want a high-performance car and have the money, you will buy a Mercedes rather than a Saturn or a Taurus or a Volkswagen. But this applies only to a restricted group of consumers.

I have had serious, and occasionally loud, arguments about this with people who run environmentally conscious companies. For instance, Jeffrey Hollender, who runs Seventh Generation, will tell you with pride that he won't sell to Wal-Mart and will offer a number of cogent and logical arguments why consumers are willing to spend that extra 5–20 percent on organic products.

Unfortunately, his arguments work beautifully in an ideal world, not the everyday world of the average American consumer. Seventh Generation is one of the largest manufacturers of eco-friendly cleaning products in America, with annual sales of over $100 million. While this is a highly respectable achievement, this growth has been achieved over twenty-five years and it is unlikely that Seventh Generation sales will ever come close to a single SC Johnson brand like Windex.

My disagreement with Jeff, and with many others who make green products, is that it is not enough to just offer a green choice at a premium price; the goal is to make green products at a competitive price. I believe strongly that if Jeffrey offered his products at the same price as Windex, his company would be significantly larger today—perhaps even bigger than Windex.

I've given hundreds of lectures over the past years and I always ask the audience this hypothetical question: "You walk into your local supermarket and see two displays for different brands of the same product. One holds the organic, eco-friendly, fair-wage version of that product. It costs $1.05 a bottle. Next to it is a normal version of the product processed with artificial chemicals and harvested by workers paid slave wages (it also happens to be trucked here from China). This version costs $1.00 a bottle. Assume that both versions give the same performance. Who would buy the one that costs $1.05?"

Every time I ask this question, roughly 5 percent of the people's hands go up. It's as if every audience is reading from the same script. (I also count myself in the group that wouldn't pay extra.) I've even asked this question at a recycling retreat in Vermont, where the majority of the audience wore no shoes on their feet and plenty of dreads on their heads. The result was the same.

I then ask the following question: "What if the two products were the same price? Which one would you buy then?" Again the audience seems to have been given a script—100 percent of the audience (there has never been an exception) raises a hand in support of the eco-friendly version. It seems fairly clear to me that everyone wants to buy organic, eco-friendly products, but it's equally clear that they don't want to pay more for them. That's where eco-capitalism comes in.

Environmentally conscious economists often point out that with our current form of capitalism most companies are not paying for the cost of the capital they are withdrawing from the earth. Oh, they pay people to extract the minerals, cut the trees, deplete the soil, and pump out the petroleum, but that's it. It's as if the earth were an enormous unlocked vault of infinite resources that can be turned into things that can be exchanged for money. Everyone can take whatever he or she wants as long as they pay carfare to get to the vault and haul the stuff away.

Moreover, once we exchange these items for capital, then by and large after using them we throw them into landfills or burn them. The eco-capitalist sees the value in this garbage. Properly reused (or upcycled), these things can continue to be exchanged for money. Like the capitalists who used the raw materials that the earth has given up so freely, eco-capitalists use this new form of raw material—to make money.

CHAPTER 6

And Then It Clicked

Part of the story of TerraCycle is learning to redefine, even to rethink words and ideas that are used every day. At TerraCycle we are constantly rethinking what we are. We had started with the idea that we could make money from waste—initially, by hauling away people's organic waste, feeding it to the worms so they could make worm poop, which we could sell. It turned out that the most predictable part of that business model—the waste-management part—was the most dispensable part. When we refocused on worm poop, we had a product that was not only unique—it was valuable.

Then, in large part out of desperation, we'd redefined another kind of waste—used soda bottles—as something that was more than just plastic waiting to be melted down at a cost, but a packaging solution that had real value. That cascaded into a complete stream of resources that we needed for our business.

The HomeDepot.com order wasn't a big one in terms of numbers, but it was huge in showing us the benefits of major retail. It would have taken us much more time and effort to put together the same amount of sales with individual stores. What we'd been forced to realize was that small companies needed to have a new idea about how to grow their business.

The success with HomeDepot.com pointed out two things. First, success breeds success. HomeDepot.com opened doors. Now Robin and I were able to make contact with people at some of the other big stores, and at the beginning of 2004 we hit the road, trying to meet with as many big-box stores as we could to build on our newfound momentum. We hit the road to visit with Canadian Tire, Zellers, Stop & Shop, Wal-Mart Canada, QVC, Publix, Whole Foods, and many, many more.

It was a thrill. Not that we were making any money, but the idea that we were selling to Home Depot fueled our excitement. If we were going to make sales of that kind our primary business model, we needed to expand.

Robin and I had always thought that we would eventually become involved with the big-box stores, and he was always looking for things that would prepare us for the big orders. One time, he found out that he could get fifty thousand misprinted Dasani water bottle boxes at an incredibly cheap price. That is a lot of boxes. Even flattened, fifty thousand boxes takes up a lot of space. The only problem was that we had no storage space of our own—except for what we could get at the greenhouse at the EcoComplex.

Never mind. It was too good an offer for Robin to refuse, so he called up Bill and said, "Bill, I bought some boxes and you'll need to store them," without saying exactly how many. Bill, naturally, said he would find some space somewhere. A few days later, when two semitrailer truckloads pulled up to the EcoComplex, Bill didn't even know if he could get them off the trucks, much less find a place for them.

It was obvious that we needed more space. For one thing,

the three of us couldn't continue to fill orders from the Eco-Complex with paint strippers and funnels. We needed a staff, we needed storage, we needed machines—we needed a factory. Finding a factory meant finding the money for a factory. Even the ever-generous Martin Stein couldn't support the kind of expansion we were envisioning. So we would have to do a large part of it on our own.

Since we were looking for a factory even though we didn't have the money for it, we also started looking for a staff that wouldn't require a salary. That was not quite as impossible as it sounds. We'd always had my friends involved here and there, people I'd met at Princeton or elsewhere and convinced that TerraCycle would not only be fun but valuable. I guess you could call them interns, although in some ways I would have counted myself in that description. The advantage to interns was that they didn't expect to be paid at all, except in experience. Every year thousands of students across America beg to work for free in exchange for a line on the résumé. We had lots of experience to share—from shoveling worm poop to bottling to selling. Every kind of job was available and ready for an eager person to grab—whether they knew what to do or not.

During the end of the school year in 2004 we went on a massive intern recruiting spree led by Alex Salzman, our lead intern. We held weekly meetings in the office on Nassau Street, where we'd pitch people on the exciting world that TerraCycle had to offer. Ten to fifteen people would show up almost every week. We promised them everything we could think of—from a mansion to live in to a butler to feed them—none of which we had at the time. By the beginning of summer 2004, we had thirty-five interns ready, eager, and willing. With a month to go, we still didn't have a home to house the students, office space for them to work in, or that elusive butler.

By this time, I was pretty tired of living in the office, so I needed a place to live anyway. It seemed like a natural combination to get a place where I could house the interns as well as live there myself. If it seems like I was trying to live in a frat house, remember where I had been living for the past year.

I had a budget of roughly $1,500 per month to pay for a place to house over thirty-five people. Princeton wasn't even close to an option. Going north only meant higher prices. So our only option, really, was going south. Which is what Trenton had been doing for decades.

If you had to find a human equivalent of discarded soda bottles, it would be America's inner cities: there are no jobs, schools are bad, property values are low, and so on and so on and so on. Trenton, New Jersey, is one such place.

At one time, Trenton was one of America's proudest and most bustling cities, with a long history. It was the scene of George Washington's first victory in the Revolutionary War, when he crossed the Delaware River at night on December 26, 1776, and surprised the British mercenary troops in Trenton. The city was the new nation's capital for a couple of months in 1784, was considered as the site of America's permanent capital, but the South objected. It remains the capital of New Jersey. The first basketball game ever was played there in 1896.

During the early 1900s, Trenton was a major center of the American Industrial Revolution, housing such companies as Roebling Steel, the company formed by the builders of the Brooklyn Bridge, and many more. It was one of the country's fifty largest cities and a booming manufacturing center for steel, rubber, wire, rope, linoleum, and ceramics. The city adopted the slogan "Trenton Makes, the World Takes" in the 1920s. The 1931 *Industrial Directory of New Jersey* proudly listed four hundred businesses with five or more employees in Trenton.

You'd be lucky to find forty now. Manufacturing started to decline in the 1950s, and people started to leave the city. By 1960 it had dropped off the list of America's one hundred largest cities. Savage riots followed Martin Luther King's assassination in 1968. In the 1970s, heroin took over the economy and the society while gangs, especially the Bloods and the Crips, took over the streets. The Bloods are a major part of the cartel that controls heroin in Trenton, as well as a substantial part of the statewide heroin traffic.

All this within ten minutes of one of the richest zip codes in America.

By the time we started to look at houses in Trenton, the population was 85,000, and maybe a third of all the buildings in the city were abandoned. Most of the jobs in the city were provided by the government. There was no artistic area, no place that would be a basis for rejuvenation. The property values had plummeted. Trenton was (and remains) the fourth most dangerous city of under 100,000 people in the United States.

Which made Trenton the best real estate option we could find. Although no new houses had been built in Trenton (outside of low-income housing) for fifty years, there were some extraordinary houses left over from Trenton's glory days. Ultimately, I found a house on Greenwood Avenue, which had once been called "millionaires' row." It had seven thousand square feet and a dozen bedrooms. But the city was so depressed that after I bought the house someone offered more for the materials in the house than I had paid for it.

Hanging from the street sign on the corner nearby were two bandannas, one red and the other blue. That was my introduction to the Bloods and the Crips. We were on the border between two gangs that were sworn enemies. In fact, one of the previous owners had been the heroin kingpin of Trenton. There was a murder in the house right next door, which was used to traffic heroin, and once shots went through the upstairs window. Not because they were shooting at us; we just happened to be in the line of fire.

I didn't know about the dimension of crime and violence in Trenton when I moved in, and luckily no one else did, either. I had that house, filled with over thirty-five interns, for two years, but no one was ever injured or threatened.

We moved into the house just when the school year at Princeton was ending, which was a bonanza for us. Most students at Princeton live on campus, but they have to furnish their rooms themselves. When they graduate, they generally just put the furniture out on the street to be thrown away. Naturally, other people's garbage was our raw materials, and we were able to furnish the Trenton house almost completely with discards from Princeton. The house had been modernized a bit by the previous owner, who had used it as a clinic, so we didn't have to repair the interior. What we did do was turn it into a place where everyone could have some fun, since it was impossible to leave the house without running into drug dealers or prostitutes on crack.

We even found that butler. When we were doing the art parties in the office, there was a guy named Tronix who would make smoothies. He became our butler, or at least our cook. It didn't really matter to us that the only thing he really knew how to make was fried chicken, so that became our nightly dinner—fried chicken and smoothies. During that first summer, we turned the basement into a combination pool room, movie theater, and keg room. As you can imagine, it was used very heavily. The interns partied just about every night until two or later.

That meant that I had to get them up in the morning. In the beginning I would go around to each room and wake people up personally—three or four people to a room. There were times when I was physically wrestled to the ground by an intern who wanted to emphasize the fact that he wasn't ready to get up that morning. After a couple of weeks, I got tired of being their personal wake-up call, so I tried other methods. Nothing worked too well until I installed enormous loudspeakers on every floor and blasted the most obnoxious music I could find as loud as possible (from Vanilla Ice to the Village People).

Since there was only one shower in the entire house, and it always ran out of hot water before everyone could use it, we had to schedule showers on a rotation—and the last unfortunate intern had to clean out all the curly little hairs that congregated by the drain hole.

Breakfast was pretty much a free-for-all, and then we'd carpool into work. About half the team would go to the office on Nassau Street, while some went to the greenhouse to shovel worm poop or bottle and label orders. We also had a team working on a lawn service—the idea was that we would use the worm poop on the lawns we serviced, so there was a natural synergy there. Unfortunately, it never quite got off the ground, given the competition from more established (and better equipped) companies—not to mention the interns' weakness for hijinks on the customers' properties. We tried it for a couple of years, but then closed it.

There was always somebody in the office until late, and somewhere along the line we discovered that the Panera Bread Co. restaurant in Princeton always threw out the day's bread and pastries after they closed at ten o'clock. So whoever was working late would stop there and leave with bags and bags of bread that had been baked the same day.

The interns really did everything that a paid staff would do, and as happens with volunteer employees (or any employees, after all), some were terrible, some did what was asked of them, and some were creative and dedicated. It was a wonderful and exhausting ride. When I wasn't traveling, I was supervising—sixteen hours a day. That was particularly difficult because all the interns were my peers.

For all the difficulties, the interns made a huge difference that summer. In order to move the TerraCycle Plant Food off the virtual shelves at HomeDepot.com, they called everyone they knew—their friends, their families, the media, local stores, garden clubs—anywhere and everywhere they could think of. And gradually over the summer it became clear that TerraCycle Plant Food became a real success. HomeDepot.com reordered. TerraCycle Plant Food was the fastest-selling plant food on HomeDepot.com!

That made it all the more urgent that we find a factory, because if we really started to make it with the big-box stores, we would have to scale up production significantly. Since the only order we had was from HomeDepot.com, buying a factory was a major risk.

We researched the properties around Princeton and found them to be completely out of the question due to their prices. But as soon as I saw the prices we could get in Trenton, we realized that was where we wanted to be. Not only because Trenton offered the best space for the price, but also because that was where people needed jobs. So at the end of the summer we took the risk, bought a building on New York Avenue in the northeast part of Trenton, and moved out of our basement office in Princeton.

The factory we found was on a city block, with one L-shaped building and a second rectangular one. There was some office space in the front at the bend of the L, two large open rooms on either side of that, and a loading dock in the back. It might not sound like much, but it was perfect for us at the time. There was room for the plastic swimming pools that held the vermicompost tea, room for the bottler, room for everything. In fact, it looked huge—after all, we had been doing production out of a one-hundred-square-foot space in the greenhouse!

Of course, it was full of old junk from the previous business, which was a company that distributed newspapers. There were a hundred huge metal tables, bindery equipment, and fifty derelict trucks on the property. So our first job was to clean it out.

We were moving into a poor area afflicted with gang violence—and let's face it, we were mostly white, middle-class Princeton students. Somehow we had to make a peace treaty—or at least a nonaggression pact—with the neighborhood. So we decided to capitalize on another problem that faces our communities—graffiti—and create value, social and environmental good, from it.

Our new factory was dilapidated and ugly, so we put the word out that people could paint our factory whenever they wanted. It started with Leon Rainbow, who was a graffiti and body artist whom I had first met during the parties in the office on Nassau Street the year before.

Most people think of graffiti as something like garbage. They think graffiti is something that defaces buildings and other structures. Moreover, they pay to have it removed, like any piece of trash! For the artists, this meant that society was out to destroy their means of expression. So when I bought the factory in Trenton, I got in touch with Leon and asked him to bring his crew around to paint the building. The response was amazing—the graffiti artists transformed the outside of the building. Today our building is repainted every month with brand-new art. For free!

In the meantime, Robin and I had played out our string of big-box store meetings, at least for that season. HomeDepot.com was still going strong, but we didn't have any other orders in sight—just one last meeting with Wal-Mart Canada.

Robin and I had been calling Wal-Mart constantly. Finally, at the beginning of the fall, someone picked up the phone. It's funny. Robin remembers that I was the one who finally made actual human contact. And I remember that it was him. Whoever it was, we probably made contact because the buyer just couldn't stand to hear our message on his machine anymore. We set up a first meeting and made our pitch with the computer presentation and the bottles of TerraCycle Plant Food and all the other paraphernalia we could carry there (including the worms).

The buyer suggested that we talk to Wal-Mart Canada and set up a meeting with the primary buyer for garden supplies, in Toronto. This was the big moment. Everyone told us that no matter what, it would not be more than a fifteen-minute meeting. Even if he liked us, fifteen minutes was the absolute tops. Five minutes if he didn't.

When we walked into the meeting—me in a John Deere

hat and Robin in his khakis—we both felt that the buyer was ready to show us the door at the very first opportunity. He was not exactly hostile, but his attitude made it perfectly clear that he was just meeting with us so he could tell us to drop off the face of the earth.

We had asked Bill to give us three of the biggest, juiciest tomatoes he could find in our gardens in the EcoComplex. When we walked in, we didn't say anything, just put the tomatoes on the table and sat down. The buyer looked us over and finally asked, "So what are the tomatoes for?" He wasn't allowed to accept gifts from vendors, which we knew.

Robin said, "We wanted you to see what an amazing job our plant food can do on vegetables. Aren't those the most beautiful tomatoes you've ever seen?" The buyer looked noncommittal. "And the other reason is that, if you don't like what we have to offer you this morning, you can throw the tomatoes at us."

That broke the ice. Thirty minutes later, he was still fascinated with us. He loved the whole idea of a product that was made of waste and was packaged in waste and especially that it wasn't at a premium price. He looked at us as if to say, "I thought I'd heard everything, but I was wrong." He liked us and he liked what we were trying to do. He told us he'd think about it and get back to us.

As we were getting ready to leave, he picked up the tomatoes and held them, as if he were weighing them. He said, "How much do you think these tomatoes weigh? I'd say this is about two pounds of tomatoes, wouldn't you?" I sort of nodded, wondering what he was getting at, but then he reached into his pocket and pulled out three dollar bills and gave them to me. "Thanks for the tomatoes," he said, "they look good."

All we could do was go home and wait.

The media kept helping us in surprising ways. During the summer, a Canadian television news magazine, *Venture,* began filming what would become an hour-long documentary about TerraCycle. I had always received attention in the Canadian media, and once again, the idea of the company made opportunities for us that we wouldn't have had if we had done things the usual way. They filmed us all that summer and through the fall.

Then, just before Christmas, *CBS Evening News* ran a national story on us. Introducing, Dan Rather said we are "proof that the American dream is still alive." They gave us two and a half minutes and said that "the product is proving to be remarkably effective." The reporter, Jim Axelrod, ended the segment by saying that the story of TerraCycle "is a reminder about following your dreams. The pot of gold at the end of the rainbow may require dealing with a ton of crap."

The program also reported that we had landed deals with Home Depot and—Wal-Mart. And we had. Not two weeks before, Wal-Mart had placed a massive order for every store in Canada. The Canadian television crew was actually there filming when Robin received the call. Now we were ready to face the real test of TerraCycle and eco-capitalism: pulling it off in the mainstream.

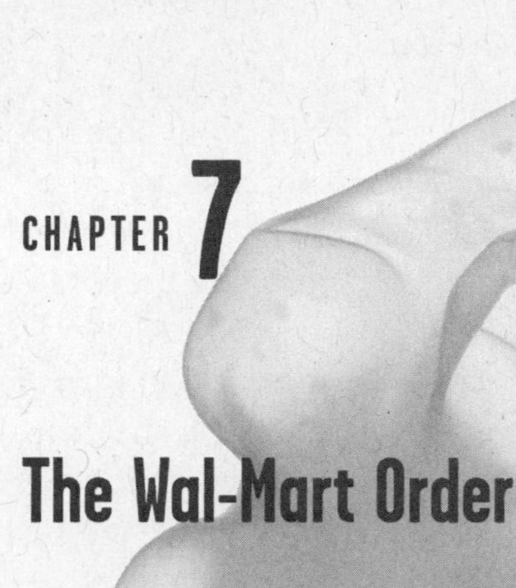

CHAPTER 7

The Wal-Mart Order

Getting the Wal-Mart order was probably the biggest thrill in the history of TerraCycle. It wasn't a dinky dot-com order, it was serious—100,000 bottles, worth over $250,000 to us. The order alone was four times bigger than our combined sales for all of 2004. Not only was it big financially, it was big for the future. We had a chance to impress the biggest retailer in the world. This could be something that would make or break TerraCycle, a chance that only comes around once in the history of a company. We had to get our game face on and make it happen. Fast!

There was just one catch. No, there were a dozen catches. We had an empty, dilapidated, inner-city factory. We were still trying to clean it up and get it ready for the worm gin and the brewing equipment and the tea vats and the bottler. We only had one worm gin to make the poop, a couple of six-foot tubs, and one rented bottling line—which didn't work all that well.

We had no staff and no equipment, no way to make the

thirty thousand gallons of worm-poop tea that the order required. On a good week at the greenhouse in 2004, we made maybe a thousand gallons a week. Which didn't include bottling and labeling and everything else. The entire order was due to be shipped no later that mid-February, which gave us two months to quadruple our production, just for starters. For that we would need more people, and on top of it the order had come in just at the beginning of the Christmas season. My few remaining interns were leaving for the holiday, and the local people were getting ready to celebrate. Oh yeah, and we were running low on cash. Very low.

The thrill was amazing, as were the massive problems that came about. We didn't have enough bottles, and we couldn't make enough worm poop ourselves. Once the reality hit it was gut-wrenching. When you're an entrepreneur, you just make decisions that seem right at the time. The scary thing is you are always making decisions without knowing the future. We sold Wal-Mart without having our infrastructure completely in place. Should we have waited to go to them until we had all the machinery and inventory we might need? What if the orders hadn't come in—we would have been broke, and without the energy boost that comes from getting something like the Wal-Mart order.

Getting the bottles was Robin's task and it nearly drove him nuts. Maybe even worse, it threatened the core of TerraCycle. When the Wal-Mart order came in, everybody but Robin and I wanted to switch to new bottles. Bill and all the rest of the team thought we should just go out and buy new bottles. We didn't really have enough money to do that, but then we didn't have any money to do anything. It wasn't the money that bothered me, it was the idea of going back to the normal way and dropping the very innovation that had saved us the last time we were almost broke.

Robin and I wanted to maintain the principle that every part of the product came from waste. We weren't entirely being obstinate about that, either, since we had seen how powerful the idea of making and packaging a product out of waste was. Once you started to dilute it, it would lose its magic.

On the other hand, we were not entirely sure how many used soda bottles had come in from the school program over the past year. It was almost impossible to tell. At one point we had filled up all the space that was available in the greenhouse—imagine a room about fifty feet wide by one hundred feet long, filled to a depth of about three feet with used soda bottles. How were we supposed to know how many bottles there were? We didn't have any time to waste, so we began with the bottles from the schools, and very quickly it became clear that we weren't going to have close to enough.

Then Robin visited every recycling center near Trenton. No luck. As a general rule, recycling centers crush all the bottles they receive because all they care about is the plastic, not the shape. For the recycler, a bottle provides plastic polymer, which is valuable (say $0.20 per pound). It also has a shape, which has negative value to the recycler. The shape is garbage, and the recycler will pay to have the shape taken out of the product—that is, a recycling center spends money destroying the shape to get to the valuable polymer.

For the eco-capitalist, the shape is as much a valuable resource as the plastic. That is, we were prepared to haul the bottles away from the recycler, who would be paid the same as when they processed the bottles. The recycling center would receive the same amount for every pound they brought in, but then we would take the bottles away so their workload was reduced. It was a win-win situation: we got usable bottles and they made a higher profit margin. That's the big bang for the buck of eco-capitalism: at the end of the day our source of bottles is the cheapest source of bottles in America! In 2008, we secured a massive order of ice melter from BJ's because the packaging cost for ice melter had risen with the increase in the cost of plastic due to the increase in the cost of fossil fuel. Because we package our ice melter in used one-gallon milk jugs, we could offer BJ's the cheapest price. As the price of fossil fuels increases—as it inevitably will—the TerraCycle model will become more and more profitable. Rising gas prices are a blessing for TerraCycle as they strengthen our competitive edge.

But in 2006 none of the recyclers were ready to change their processing routines just for us, and as far as anyone knew, just for that order. We were getting desperate. Just a few days before we would be forced to buy new bottles, Robin discovered the benefit of living near a bottle-bill state like New York. In a bottle-bill state people can return their bottles to centers and get $0.05 back per bottle.

So what's different about these state-run centers? They *don't crush the bottles*! Instead they sort them and then send the bottles to recycling centers (where they would be crushed). At the New York Recycling Center, huge trucks come in from all around the state with enormous loads of bottles. They dump their loads onto a conveyor belt, which leads to a machine that separates the plastic from metal.

This was our salvation. Robin and I met with the director of the recycling center and asked him if we could take all the twenty-ounce bottles off his hands. We told him that we would pick up the bottles as they came in and we'd buy them for the price they get *after* they do their processing. At first, he was reluctant. It was something new and it meant changing his system, and nobody likes to do that, especially someone who works for a state bureaucracy. The one drawback to our approach is that, initially, it's almost always the harder way to go. We have to invent new logistical processes to make it happen.

If we didn't get them, the Wal-Mart order would have to go out in new bottles and TerraCycle Plant Food would no longer be the only product made entirely from garbage. All those weeks of effort would have been wasted.

Finally, the director grudgingly said we could have them as long as we did all the work. "Oh, and you'll have to provide all the gaylords," he said, and turned back to his desk to make some notes.

Robin said, "Oh sure, no problem." I mouthed, "Gay lords?" to him, but he just shushed me. As soon as we got outside, I completely lost it laughing. Robin explained to me that gaylords are just giant boxes—four feet by four feet by six feet or the like; these are the kinds of things you learn, I guess.

We hired a couple of people to sort the bottles for us at the recycling center. We even drew up big pictures of exactly the kind of bottles we wanted and hung them up on the wall so that the sorters could check in case they got confused. They pulled the bottles off the belt and dropped them into a chute that would drop them into the gaylords.

The final thing was equipment. The first big problem was tanks. We needed fifteen five-hundred-gallon tanks to make enough liquid worm poop to stay on schedule. But since we were doing this entire order during the Christmas/New Year's season, no equipment manufacturer would make anything for us. Every custom tank shop had a lead time that would kill our order: eight to ten weeks.

This was my problem to solve. What object was ready to order and could hold at least five hundred gallons of water? First, I ordered some above-ground swimming pools, which came fast but didn't last. Every single one resulted in a worm-poop tsunami at our factory (with me in it). Eventually, I discovered horse-feeding troughs. They look like enormous children's swimming pools and are built to stand up to heavy use.

Once that was solved, we fired up our paint strippers and got to work—we labeled the very first thirty thousand or forty thousand bottles that way, until our newly acquired heat tunnel showed up.

At midnight on February 4, we officially started the big push. We worked fifteen days straight, seven days a week, twenty hours a day. Robin and I spent many nights sleeping in the factory, and Bill worked as hard as we did—he just didn't sleep there. We'd take naps in the front office on the floor. We didn't have the time or inclination to find a hotel in Trenton. But we pulled it off. We finished in mid-February, on time with every bottle, and collapsed. We proved at least to ourselves that eco-capitalism can work at the biggest level. We ran out of money the day the last pallet left our factory. We had to pull our accounts receivable like crazy and fund-raise like demons.

If you get the sense that we were just a bunch of guys trying anything they could think of to make it work, you'd be right. I've always learned on the job, in real time. A problem comes up, I research it and try to solve it. You can't study to be an entrepreneur; you learn by fire.

But in a way, you can learn to be an entrepreneur. All entrepreneurial experiences are related, whether you're selling worm poop to Wal-Mart or a grade-tracking application to the public elementary school system. In the end, there are enough similarities that you get used to the mind-set. I never for a moment thought that we wouldn't make the order. Not because we were heroes, but because I just don't think that way. It would be a waste of time to stop and wonder whether we were going to make it—you just get it done.

We could probably have finished sooner and with less agonizing if we had simply gone out and bought new bottles, but I still think that would have taken something very fundamental away from us. Robin and I believed that, ultimately, we would have the best return on investment if we stuck to the model—finding value in what other people considered waste. You would be wrong if you put more emphasis on the "eco" part or the "capitalist" part—both sides together contribute to the success of the business.

After we shipped the Wal-Mart order, publicity in Canada just exploded. There were articles in all the major newspapers and business papers. CBC's hour-long documentary about us, ending with Robin's call to me about the Wal-Mart order, was broadcast just as we were finishing up the order. Since they had been there when everything was happening, they had lots of "fantastic" footage. They even had me dress up in a kind of superhero costume, as Wormboy. This is the kind of thing you do when you want your company to survive at any cost.

On top of all this we had fantastic luck with our timing. In 2004, the City of Toronto enacted a very controversial bylaw intended to encourage home owners to avoid using synthetic chemical products to kill lawn weeds and bugs. By 2005, about seventy Canadian cities had passed laws that either banned or restricted the use of pesticides for lawn care.

TerraCycle Plant Food fit perfectly into the new awareness of environmentally friendly products. The Wal-Mart spokesman, Kevin Groh, told the *Toronto Globe and Mail* that TerraCycle Plant food would be "something we're not tucking away in a corner of the store." We were the subject of dozens of news articles and suddenly there was interest from all kinds of stores that had never picked up the phone before.

Once we started getting new orders, it became pretty obvious that we needed more help. To begin with, for instance, a receptionist. As it was, people could wander into the factory and we'd be in the back fixing one thing or another. Once she joined our team we could set up to hire more people, so we put a two-line ad in the newspaper. The ad was for the most basic work in the factory—bottling, boxing, cleaning, things like that. There were four or five positions in all, and they all paid minimum wage (which was more than Robin and I were making so far). People were supposed to apply in person on Monday. Robin came down from Toronto on Sunday night to help me interview.

That morning as we drove in together we saw a huge line. It just kept going and going. I turned to Robin and said, "The hospital must be hiring, too." Then we passed the hospital and the line was still going. The TerraCycle factory was another three blocks down the road.

Robin turned to me and said, "Tom, I think this line is for us." And we looked at each other in a panic—if it was for us, how were we possibly going to handle all these people? I said,

"No, no, it can't possibly be. No one knows who we are or what we're doing." But the line kept going until it stretched right into TerraCycle's front door. Robin said to me, "Don't worry, don't worry. We have the receptionist now. She'll take care of things until we can get settled."

We parked the car down the street, pulled out the small stack of applications we'd just copied—I think I went all out and made twenty-five of them—and went into the factory, sidestepping all the people waiting to get in, telling them that we'd take care of them in just a few minutes, take it easy, we'd be back, and so forth. We hustled into the front of the factory—you could call it the reception area, but you'd really be overstating the case. There was basically a desk in front of a doorway that was straight down the hall from the front door.

As we walked up to the receptionist's desk, she stood up and screamed at us, "You guys are *nuts*!" and shook her fists in the air in frustration. "I quit!" And she stomped out the front door.

I looked at Robin. "What are we going to do now?"

Without missing a beat, Robin said, "You know, I bet you there's a receptionist in that line somewhere." So we sat down at the desks that we'd scrounged from the trash and started taking applications.

Since we were broke again until Wal-Mart paid us—which wasn't going to be for another month or two—we hit the road for more investment. Martin Stein, as always, contributed substantially, but thankfully other new investors also joined the party, and by May we had $1.5 million raised. Just as important, May was the end of the school year at Princeton, and we had a new wave of interns coming into the Trenton house.

That was not only a boon to the business, it was a relief to me. I had spent the whole winter in the massive Trenton house and was very sketched out. Soyeon wouldn't even come to visit me since she was so petrified about being there. It was so incredibly big, I never knew where sounds were coming from, and in that neighborhood I could never know what the sounds meant. Occasionally, there would be interns to keep me company, even as many as ten, but I spent a lot of time alone there, too. If I hadn't been working such long hours, I might have started sleeping in the office again.

The money and the new interns arrived just in time. We sent them out to visit every Wal-Mart store in Canada—from Halifax to British Columbia—to teach the associates about our products. They did a terrific job, and soon we were selling incredibly well.

Then another up: our big-box hunt bagged the biggest game in the fertilizer industry of all, a meeting with Home Depot USA. In April 2005, I was able to convince Eric Smith, an advisor at the time, to get me into a meeting with the main fertilizer buyer for Home Depot, John Fuller. As usual, everyone told me that it would be a fifteen-minute meeting at best.

I showed up in the lobby of Home Depot in Atlanta in my usual T-shirt and John Deere cap. This is the first time Eric and I met face-to-face and I could see he was shocked. After looking me up and down he told me not to say anything, that he would do all the talking.

That meeting, like that first one at Wal-Mart, lasted an hour—Eric never said a word. Fuller was as fascinated with the model and with the presentation as everyone else was. In fact, so was Eric. Four months later he quit his job and came to TerraCycle to be the vice president of sales.

Home Depot agreed to test our poop in stores in New Jersey in August 2005. That was our first big break in bricks-and-mortar stores in the United States. That year, we increased our sales by more than 500 percent and finished the year with $450,000 in sales.

Our sales didn't grow in a steady, gentle upward grade. We would get a big order, fulfill it, catch our breaths, and then we would get another big order. I'm sure that Bill came near to killing me several times that year. I worried constantly that we wouldn't have enough product to meet the demand of the big-box stores, so I was constantly pushing for him to increase production. That meant getting more and bigger everything. We scrounged two five-thousand-gallon tanks from the landfill for the brewing. They were so big we couldn't even get them into the factory. We had to cut off the tops before we could bring them inside.

In addition to the equipment, Bill was always looking for new sources of worm poop. We called every worm farmer we could find to see if they would sell us their poop. It turned out that a lot of them had been caught up in the old B&B Ponzi scheme. Naturally, they were more than happy to finally find a buyer for their compost. One farmer in the South was particularly well stocked.

But the problem was that each lot of worm poop had a slightly different composition. Bill ended up developing a secret recipe from a combination of different types of worm poop. He had to mix them, test them, mix them again.

Luckily, everything we did that year seemed to work.

Later that year, in June 2006, *Inc.* magazine did a cover story that called us "the coolest little start-up in America." It became one of the best-selling covers for *Inc.* that year. We had no idea that we would be on the cover, much less that they would invent a new category for us. The article was a terrific advertisement for the product, saying that it was as effective as the big-name commercial plant foods on the market, but it also pointed to the real reason we were successful: "At the moment, TerraCycle seems to have everything going for it. And yet, looking at it today, you would never guess how often the company has come close to failing. On each occasion, however, an angel appeared in time to rescue Szaky and his project. In the end, TerraCycle proved to be the company that refused to die—and a case study in the power of a big idea."

A month later, Zerofootprint, an organization that aims to help people measure the size of their carbon footprint on the environment, declared TerraCycle Plant Food the first consumer product to win its seal of approval. We were the only product they had surveyed that has substantially no negative effect on the environment.

Between the publicity and the visibility in the marketplace, and the new money, our sales went through the roof. Our sales had gone from $70,000 in 2004 to $1.5 million in 2006. The factory that had seemed so huge when we walked in was now beginning to look small.

Then in early 2007 we landed Target, Whole Foods, Kroger, Wal-Mart USA, and a number of other big accounts. We launched new flavors of worm poop: orchid and African violet plant foods, concentrated lawn fertilizer, concentrated liquid garden fertilizer, potting mix, and seed starter. We were on track for more than doubling sales again to $3.5 million. We were taking off!

It was perfect.

CHAPTER 8

suedbyscotts.com

It was like a nightmare that you couldn't wake up from. On March 6, 2007, Scotts Miracle-Gro, the largest plant food company in the United States, delivered a lawsuit against us in every possible way. First it came by e-mail. Then it was hand-delivered by a messenger. Then it came by registered mail. It felt like it just kept coming and coming and there was no way to stop it. The 173-page document said that we were falsely advertising that TerraCycle Plant Food "outgrows the leading synthetic fertilizer" and that our packaging—what the business calls our trade dress—resembled that of Miracle-Gro too closely.

What made it worse was that our legal counsel, Rick Ober, wasn't available. In fact, he was on a plane flying to Marysville, Ohio. Why Marysville? Because it's Scotts's U.S. headquarters, and Rick was going there to meet with the Scotts legal people.

The suit was not the first time we had heard from Scotts. In 2006, they had notified us that they had concerns about our packaging and our advertising. We were a little surprised—in fact, we were a little surprised that Scotts Miracle-Gro knew we existed—but we responded right away that we were willing to work with them to address any concerns they had. We did not have the stomach for going up against this company, and we figured we would be able to come to an agreement. We had gone ahead with a new round of financing, and the signs were good that we would meet our goal of $2 million. In fact, I was expecting to be receiving an offer—and possibly even a check—that very day.

Now Scotts is an extraordinary company, one of the great success stories in American business. In fact, it is a trajectory that I only hope TerraCycle can emulate one day. It is the story of how vision, creativity, determination, and hard work can pay off. It went from being a local operation basically in one man's backyard to being a $3 billion business.

Scotts was really turned into a success by a public relations expert, Horace Hagedorn. According to a DVD biography of Hagedorn that was produced by his family and is publicly available, Hagedorn was so excited by the possibilities of Miracle-Gro, the product he was promoting, that he took on more and more responsibility for the operation of the company. Eventually, he bought out the owner and became the head of Miracle-Gro.

Miracle-Gro's main competitor was a larger company named Scotts. But Hagedorn was not going to let their size stop him. He personally produced a series of commercials with the craggy-faced actor James Whitmore that directly compared the effectiveness of Miracle-Gro to its Scotts competition. The ads were so good that Scotts finally came to Hagedorn and offered to merge the two companies.

The company gradually became the preeminent lawn food company in America, and it has tenaciously defended that position. As *Advertising Age* noted, "With a roughly 59 percent market share, Scotts dominates its business like few other brands." We weren't the first company that Scotts had sued when they felt that those companies were improperly trying to imitate some aspect of the combination of factors that has brought Scotts to the top of the heap. "Any claims about our product's effectiveness—we take them very seriously," said a Scotts spokesperson. "I think anyone who is starting and growing a company would understand. It's common sense, Business 101." Maybe they meant I should have stayed at Princeton longer.

I had not had the slightest inclination to misappropriate any of Scotts's characteristics. It seemed to me that used soda bottles were recognizably different from the Scotts containers. I agree that we used green and yellow as part of our packaging, and I can only point out that as the colors of the sun and grass, they are widely used by a number of companies. Still, I was prepared to change them before the suit and now will be changing them as part of the settlement of the lawsuit. Indeed, there are a number of things I'd like to say in praise of Scotts that I am barred from saying by the settlement.

When the lawsuit hit (and hit and hit) my desk, I have to say that I was scared. We were just making our way into the big stores and sales were terrific. But I knew that a prolonged lawsuit could stop us in our tracks. On the one hand there was the cost, which could easily run up to $1 million if it went on for a long time—and a year is not uncommon. There are all kinds of costs that go into fighting a lawsuit. You have to hire local counsel in addition to your own lawyer. You have to provide copies of just about every piece of paper and e-mail that is in or has gone out of the office. This is part of the process of discovery, and gives the plaintiff the opportunity to see if there has been any concerted effort to imitate the plaintiff's products or packaging and the like. This is certainly a crucial part of the legal system, but it can be expensive, not only in materials, but especially in the staff time it takes. The costs can easily become so great that a small company can go out of business.

Another problem, and one of the most difficult to fight, is the effect it has on the staff. It's incredibly unsettling and distracting for people—they can't help but worry whether they will have a job at the end of the day, and that's depressing. And if we started missing our shipping dates, we'd lose the credibility and trust we were starting to build up with these tough retailers.

So there were all kinds of reasons for me to be worried. It was incredibly difficult telling the people in the office. I sent out an e-mail with the basic facts, but then I went around to everyone individually and tried to reassure them that we would do the best we could for them and for the company. The last thing we wanted to do was fight this to the bitter end. What we wanted, in fact, was a short, sweet resolution. My first thought when I looked at the lawsuit was, How the hell do I fight this?

However, I think anyone who wants to start their own company or be part of running a company needs to realize that probably some kind of make-or-break situation will hit you before you have things working the way you want. There's never a good time for a lawsuit or a flood or a strike or any of the other things that can spell the end for a small company. You won't be able to predict it and you won't be able to prepare for it—because you just don't know what it might be. The only way to prepare is to make sure that you're ready to bounce back when something knocks you to the floor.

What is amazing, though, is that in the course of bouncing back you may discover strengths you didn't know you had. Or, as in our case, you may find that the fight itself is an advantage. I can say with some confidence now that if Scotts hadn't sued us, we wouldn't be doing as well as we are.

So I was disappointed that Scotts had decided not to work with us, and naturally I was very worried about what might happen. I was finally able to talk to Rick and plan some strategy. The first thing was to make sure that no one made any untoward public remarks about the suit or Scotts, so we decided that only I, our marketing director, and our publicist, Albert Zakes, would speak for TerraCycle publicly.

Albe, as he prefers to be known, had only come to the company six months before, and he almost didn't. The previous fall, we had put a help-wanted listing for a publicist on Craigslist.com, after the media wave had really started to peak and was about to crash down on us. Albe was an environmentalist who had been working for a public interest research group in Colorado, where he had gone to college.

After our first interview with Albe, he didn't seem a perfect fit—since he had no direct experience in publicity—and we said thanks, but no thanks. But then he wrote me a long and impassioned letter about why he wanted to work at TerraCycle and what he could bring to the job that other people with more experience would not. He was so committed to the idea of TerraCycle and so enthusiastic that I had to believe he was worth a try. Part of TerraCycle's model is repurposing perfectly good things. So Albe was our point person, and the point only got sharper when the marketing director left not long after.

In addition to our staff, I had to let our prospective investors know about the suit. I had no idea whether they would decline to continue the process, wait until it had played itself out, or just walk away.

What about our customers? Would they be wary of dealing with us because of the suit? I'm sure that some were, but not all of them. Around that time, I had to go to a sales meeting for suppliers for Home Depot Canada. The media had been invited to this particular one, and *Maclean's,* one of Canada's most enduring and popular magazines, did a colorful story on the meeting:

> Around 2 p.m., the room shifts to a state of heightened alertness. All eyes turn toward the main entrance, where a svelte blond has appeared. It's Annette Verschuren, president of Home Depot Canada. Like dolphins at feeding time, the salesmen all angle for some bit of attention. Soon, Verschuren's gaze falls on the rumpled plant-food salesman. "Tom Szaky!" she exclaims, leaning in for an air-kiss. "Have you seen our new *Eco-Options* magazine?"

> "Absolutely," says Szaky. "It's great."
>
> "You have anything new to show me?"
>
> Szaky hands her a plastic bottle of his new spray-nozzle lawn fertilizer. "The spray nozzle—nice touch," she says. "Any innovative products, Tom, you should always consider test-marketing them with us." Verschuren inclines her head at an underling. "We should do an interview with Tom for the *Eco-Options* magazine." Then the executive gives Szaky one last look and says, "You really should come to work for us some day."

Embarrassing as the article was, I was relieved to discover that our major customers continued to deal with us as they always had.

Nonetheless, we had to find a way to fight back. It was obvious that we couldn't outlawyer Scotts. They had deep pockets and were clearly prepared to stand their ground. We would run out of money before we could beat them in the courts. So that wasn't an option. Rick, of course, would keep doing what he did so well, but other than letting Rick fight it out with Scotts, what could we do?

We were back on TerraCycle's home ground, so to speak. No money and no power. For anybody born after 1980, the answer in such cases is obvious: the Internet. We started a Web site, suedbyscotts.com, that was intended to get our side of the story out. Probably most people hadn't heard of TerraCycle, so they wouldn't know if we were a giant, shadowy, global conglomerate or space aliens. It presented the facts of the two companies, such things as their relative size, pictures of their trade dress and ours, what we had said in our advertising and why, and the like. It had both the Scotts complaint and our response.

But a Web site is no good unless people know about it to go there, so we had to get media attention. We thought about hiring an outside PR firm, but in my opinion PR firms are more in the business of getting a monthly retainer and less in the business of getting you press.

So we did it ourselves. In fact, Albe was eager to do it, because he felt that the big guy versus little guy story would be a very strong angle for journalists. The headline of the release drove home the point that we were a "Small, Eco-Friendly Organic Company Started by Students." We pointed out that our bottles were recycled, collected by "children in communities across the land," and that we donated five cents to a nonprofit of their choice. We said that if we went under, inner-city jobs would be lost. And we directed people to the Web site.

Hey, we weren't trying to be evenhanded. We wanted to give the media a gut-grabbing story that had plenty of angles for them to work. Many journalists are overworked, and if you can give them a prepackaged story, you're golden. Most press releases are boring, long, and don't really frame the story in an effective way—and sometimes they avoid it altogether. A killer press release is one that the publisher can print word for word, with quotes and photos, if it chooses. But most of all, it's all about the headline. The headline will make or break your release.

Naturally, the release went everywhere, but the first responses were with our core friends: environmental groups, schools, and the vast range of environmentally conscious groups on the Web. The bottle brigade program helped terrifically.

At the end of March, Philadelphia's Wissahickon Charter School became the two thousandth school to join the bottle brigade and we agreed to supply enough fertilizer to keep the meadow in front of the school green. Some schools near Atlanta had to use a trailer to send us their bottles because people were donating them in such huge numbers. We had collected nearly a million and a half used bottles.

What made the bottle brigade important was that it put our name in hundreds of local papers around the country. Just about every time we started in a school, the local paper would do a story on us. And it gave us allies in communities all over. It didn't hurt that March was the start of the gardening season, so newspapers were doing stories on our products—as well as our competitors' products—anyway. All in all, TerraCycle's name was more visible than it ever had been.

So we thought we had a good story, but we still had to sell it. Writers get hundreds of e-mails a day and may not read your press release. So you have to call and get them on the phone. Once you're on the phone, you have to care about the story and be passionate about it in order to make them care.

One of our first big breaks came because of an old friend, the Tigernet. I discovered that there was a Princeton alum working at the *Wall Street Journal,* obviously one of our prime targets. I asked Albe to call her up, and she was fascinated with TerraCycle and what was happening. She wrote an article that started on the front page of the *Journal*'s second section. The article pointed out that our "overall company sales for the four weeks since the online campaign launched surged 122 percent from the immediately previous four weeks. Last year, the company's sales increased 31 percent in the same period. Meantime, TerraCycle's main Web site, which averages about a thousand visitors a day, has spiked as high as thirteen thousand, according to the company."

We weren't exactly celebrating, though indeed the response to the Web site and the increased sales had improved the morale of the people on the production line. But we were hardly out of the woods. As the *Journal* article pointed out, "no amount of public appeal can help TerraCycle escape the realities of litigation. As part of the discovery process, Scotts has asked for extensive documentation from TerraCycle, including everything relating to product development, contracts with retailers, strategic business plans, as well as details about 'the composition of the materials consumed by the worms.'"

Still, though, we also wanted to get a story on the national newswires. The Associated Press has a bureau office in Trenton, and they had done a story about the founding of TerraCycle a couple of years ago that really increased our visibility at the time when it was still pretty low. We sent them the press kit, we e-mailed, and we called and called and called. No response. Albe, who was suffering through serious on-the-job training, didn't have any connections there, and we didn't have a fully equipped publicity contact list. It was like beating your head against a stone wall.

Finally, I said to Albe that he should just go down to the Trenton office and make them listen to him. We didn't really have anything to lose, after all. So he did, and what happened was priceless.

He walked into the AP building, and of course there was a security guard there. Her job was basically to keep everyone who didn't work there out. Newspapers are always swamped with people, both sane and crazy, who think that the world should know their story, so the security people are there to keep things secure. And there was Albe, looking like a postcollege kid carrying plant food and a bunch of literature from us. It was no go. Albe chatted, suggested, cajoled, wheedled, and finally pleaded with her to let him see somebody. A reporter, an assistant, anybody. Nothing.

Finally, it was time for the guards to change shifts, so a new guard came up and asked what was going on. "Who are you from?" she asked. When Albe said he was representing TerraCycle, the new guard said, "Oh yeah, my sister uses that on her flowers. She says it's terrific." She turned to the first guard. "Let's let him in." And they did.

He pitched the story to an AP editor, who, like most people who hear our story, was fascinated with the business model, the product, and the personal stories. Albe's commitment to TerraCycle carried the day; the AP did a story, and now we had a truly national media campaign—all without spending a dime.

Ironically, the AP story made it into the *Columbus Dispatch,* Scotts's hometown newspaper. They called us "the little green plant-product company." There was also an article in the *Columbus Business First* that began, "It's no longer a big deal when Marysville-based Scotts Miracle-Gro Co. sues. With hundreds of patents and trademarks to defend, lawyers for Scotts are kept working pretty busy." Then it described our Internet-based defense, mentioned the Web site, and concluded, "The basic strategy, it seems, is to shame Scotts into withdrawing its lawsuit. We'll bet worm poop to corporate jets that's not going to happen."

Well, that depends on your point of view. The legal wrangling went on all summer. During that time, we closed our third round of financing for $2 million. Those investors didn't seem bothered by the suit. We vastly expanded the product line, adding plant food for roses, tomatoes, cactus, and tropical plants, as well as offering new sizes.

At the same time, the bottle brigade program was expanding by leaps and bounds. A Little League team in New Jersey started collecting bottles. A school in Ohio began collecting bottles to save an orangutan habitat in Borneo. The kinds of groups were also spreading across the board, as well as what they were collecting for. In Delaware, they were recycling for the Delaware Autism School. The Djole Dance & Drum Company in North Charleston, Virginia, collected bottles to contribute to fighting AIDS in Africa.

Local newspapers almost inevitably did a story about whatever group in their area was collecting bottles and why. The result was an incredible synergy whenever we introduced TerraCycle Plant Food anywhere around the country. In July, the Kroger supermarket chain tested our product in stores from Nevada to Ohio, and there were dozens of articles in every state. The combination of the suit, our product, and the bottle brigade brought us publicity and visibility that was probably worth every penny—and there were a lot of them—that we spent on our legal defense.

In September, those costs finally ended. We came to an agreement with Scotts.

So after six months of sound and fury, what had Scotts

gained by its suit? TerraCycle was now much more recognizable across the country and enormous numbers of environmentally concerned gardeners and bloggers were aware of how it worked. Many said they would stop using Scotts and switch to TerraCycle Plant Food just because they felt the suit was unnecessary and unfair. We had been the subject of more than 30 million media hits, including five articles in the *Wall Street Journal,* two in the *New York Times,* and articles in the *Chicago Tribune,* the *Boston Globe,* the *Los Angeles Times,* the *San Francisco Chronicle,* the BBC *World News,* and many, many more. If we had had to pay for that kind of attention, it would have cost easily more than $5 million.

We were now the best-known organic fertilizer product in the country. We finished 2007 at $3.3 million in sales. We had national distribution in Home Depot, Wal-Mart, Target, and a number of other major retailers. We were in hundreds more stores than we had been in at the beginning of the year. The bottle brigade was at work in thirty-seven hundred locations across the country. While the lawsuit was raging, we opened a round of investment for $5 million and closed within a few weeks of opening it.

We came out of the lawsuit stronger than we had gone into it, but I'm not sure what Scotts got out of it. If our roles had been reversed, I would have asked my team to invest the money that would be spent on pursuing legal action into making our products better. Which is not to disparage Scotts products, of course; they are perfectly good. But there is no limit to how good a product can get, no such thing as a perfect product. If our company becomes big in that way, we would try to buy out our competitors first. If that didn't work, we would try to make our products competitive.

What is interesting is that just as Scotts was trying to check our encroachment on their business model, we were once again revolutionizing our business model. We were pleased with the growth of the plant food products, but I became more and more interested in other ways of applying the TerraCycle model—of finding new ways to use things that other people will pay you to dispose of—to entirely different kinds of products. Can the model be applied to any other kinds of waste? How about every other kind of waste? What were the limits, if there were any? Since we had cornered the market on worm poop, why not find out?

CHAPTER 9

Why Can't Everything Be Made from Waste?

In the four short years of its life, TerraCycle had been a constantly evolving idea. After that "Aha!" moment in Montreal, the company had been about waste management. We would undercut other waste haulers because we would use it to feed worms rather than building a modern landfill—which is a complicated, highly regulated project.

Then we saw the elegance of using waste to feed worms whose waste would be our primary product. TerraCycle had discovered a fundamental thing: that what other people considered waste could also be considered a raw material. Waste from the dining halls was feed for our worms. Waste from the worms was a highly effective plant food.

So in the process of launching TerraCycle Plant Food we inadvertently created a new paradigm for consumer products. We proved that because our product is both extremely environmentally responsible (probably the most responsible) and extremely socially responsible, it can retail for an affordable price and succeed in the world's biggest retailers. The benefits to society are not by-products of the process. In fact, they actually help keep the price low. This was a feat that had eluded most environmentally friendly products.

We had also discovered that doing things our way was almost always harder in the beginning because we had to invent whole new supply chains—we were, in effect, rerouting a channel that usually went into the landfill so that it would instead flow into our factory. That led to the second "Aha!" moment, when we saw that the soda bottles people were discarding, or perhaps recycling, were also a perfectly good raw material. We had always been Dumpster diving for our office furniture, but that was the first time we realized that greatly expanding our Dumpster diving could fuel our production line. We had discovered that contemporary America is a vast Dumpster of industrial products that manufacturers are constantly throwing away or recycling—even when they're in perfect condition. That opened the floodgates for TerraCycle, and discarded spray tops, packing material, and so forth. But there was much more. Just as an example, one major retailer in America throws out over 35 million gift cards annually because the artwork didn't sell. That's forty-two full trucks of gift cards.

In looking at waste as an entirely modern, man-made idea, I stopped viewing garbage as garbage and instead slowly started to see it as a commodity. A commodity with some very unique characteristics: it has negative or very low value (typically people pay to dispose of it), it is always a by-product of some other function, it is all around us, it is created in almost every part of our lives, and there is a tremendous amount of it (much more than you would ever imagine). Since 1960, the amount of waste generated in America by consumers alone has nearly tripled, to over 250 million tons per year. That's almost one ton per person. It's no surprise that America's biggest export by weight is waste. There are hundreds of different waste streams out there, and many of them are almost completely hidden from the consumer's view. So much waste has been wantonly discarded in the oceans that there is an accumulation of floating plastics the size of Texas slowly swirling in the Pacific. This gyre has been dubbed the Asian Trash Trail, the Trash Vortex, or the Eastern Garbage Patch.

Part of the reason I started looking at the world of waste differently is that we were beginning to hit a wall with TerraCycle Plant Food. Even with all the new lines we were offering, the simple fact is that the plant food market, especially the liquid plant food market, is small. It's a tenth of the size of the solid fertilizer market, which is a tenth of the size of, say, the home cleaning product market. If we were going to become a billion-dollar company, we would need to apply our model to products beyond liquid plant food.

So it was time to reinvent ourselves again. Instead of focusing on being the most environmentally friendly plant food company on the planet, we would strive to become the most environmentally friendly consumer-product company on the planet, period. Our first step in going beyond worm poop still kept us in the garden. Was there waste we were creating that we could use? We discovered that there was.

After making the vermicompost tea, we were left with a lot of "used" worm poop. Sort of like the tea leaves that are left when you brew tea at home (except much, much more). We were, in a sense, throwing away our tea bags—but our tea leaves were still useful. (Yours are, too—you can throw them in the composter.) Though some of the nutrients leached into TerraCycle Plant Food, the used poop was still full of great stuff. So we used the used poop as the main ingredient of our seed starter and our potting mix. Both were well received, but we hadn't really leapt out of the poop.

As our focus broadened, we were on a constant lookout for ways to transform garbage into viable products. A great idea arose when I visited one of our investors, Rich Frank, who owns a vineyard in Napa Valley. One of the most important tools for making great California wine actually originates in Africa. Since both America and Europe lack a plentiful supply of domestic oak, wine-barrel makers import oak from Africa, typically shipping it to France because of its long tradition of wine-barrel construction (called cooperage). There the oak is hand-coopered into gorgeous fifty-five-gallon wine barrels and shipped around the world, notably to Napa, where it is used to ferment grapes into wine. It's no wonder that the barrels cost nearly $1,000 each!

Winemakers prefer oak barrels to reusable stainless steel barrels, since they add a flavor to the wine that is particularly delicious. But once the wine is drawn off, after their first (and only) use, these barrels are thrown out! The wine, after all, also affects the wood, and when it is exposed to air, various chemical reactions occur that would throw off the taste of new wine. So the wine barrels become waste, albeit of a particularly luxurious kind. Oh, that's cool, I thought at the time. I might be able to use that someday.

Just around the time of that visit to Rich, we had been asking our customers—Wal-Mart and Home Depot and the others—for ideas as to what they would like to see TerraCycle make next.

Soon after the lawsuit settled, Robin and I were at Home Depot pitching our products for the next selling season. The meeting was going well, and when we were almost done, I said to the buyer, "I'm sure that I can find a way to make anything out of garbage, at a better price than anyone else can make it from new materials. What are you looking for?" The buyer said that he felt there was a gap in the composter product line. They wanted a home composter that could retail at a strong price (under $200) and be more appealing than the plastic composters that had dominated the market.

Composters range from ultra-low-tech—basically a pile of kitchen and garden wastes—to very complicated containers with multiple compartments that sort of automate the mixing of the materials until they become compost. Basically, all a composter needs to do is hold organic waste material as it breaks down. It needs an opening, ideally with a door that can close securely, where you can put the waste in and take the compost out. You can speed up the process by mixing the materials up, so being able to rotate the container is also a good feature. Since it will likely be outside, it should be watertight.

Robin and Bill and I were tossing ideas back and forth, and I remembered the wine barrels. Robin agreed that they were perfect and started working on designing it.

A few days later, when I got to Toronto, I took one look at Robin's design and said, "I bet this would work better if we approached the design differently." Robin threw up his hands in frustration. For one thing, he had the barrel standing on its end. It was clear to me that if the barrel were on its side, it would be the coolest rotary composter around. We sat down and redesigned it that day, ending up with a very simple design: turn the barrel on its side, cut a hole in the end, attach a door to it, and the barrel instantly becomes a rotary composter. You could roll it with your foot. Later that day we added a simple base with four casters. Set the barrel on the casters and voilà, it rotated easily. The next day I was in Atlanta showing it to the Home Depot buyer, who loved it and agreed to test it in a large number of stores. "Oh, and by the way," the buyer said, "we're also looking for a good rain barrel—again, competitive price and better looking than the plastic ones. Lots of parts of the country are experiencing drought and people are more interested in collecting rain to water the garden. See what you can do with that."

We could do a lot with it. A wine barrel would be ideal for collecting rain, since it has the essential feature of being water-tight, can hold fifty-five gallons of liquid, is beautiful to look at, has a great story, and even smells of Napa Valley wine. All you have to do is cut a hole in the top and attach two spigots, and suddenly you have a rain barrel that is much more attractive than any plastic barrel but retails at close to the same price.

As a side note, it's funny that the two landmark events in our company started with mild intoxicants.

All we had to do was figure out how to manufacture the composters and rain barrels. At least this time, we figured, we knew where the barrels would come from, but we didn't really have anybody to do the carpentry in Trenton. We didn't want to invest a lot of money in setting up a production site, since there was always the possibility that the composter wouldn't work in the test marketing. In other words, it was the usual TerraCycle product development cycle.

We looked everywhere for a carpenter, but they didn't seem to be common in Trenton. In the middle of the search, I had to go to New York for an event for HP computers. They were doing a commercial on us—profiling TerraCycle as a small company that used HP computers for its business operations. They sent a limo down to Trenton to pick me up and take me to New York, and during the whole ride I was on the phone with Robin, talking about how hard it was to find a good carpenter. At the end of the trip, the driver turned around and said in a thick Hispanic accent, "Excuse me, sir, I know I should not have been listening to your conversation. . . ." No problem, I said, don't worry about it. "Sir, I would like to be your carpenter."

I couldn't believe it. He said that he was from Costa Rica originally and had worked as a carpenter there. Then he decided to move to the United States with his family and couldn't find anything but driving limos. I told him to come to the office and we'd talk it over.

Ron, the driver, showed up the next day and got the job.

Meanwhile, Robin had been talking to our investor who owned the winery. It turned out that he didn't turn over nearly enough barrels every year to supply us. Ironically, we had gained a carpenter and lost the wine barrels. So Robin started calling all the larger wineries, which would have a higher turnover of barrels. Since the source of wine barrels is dependent on when winemakers feel that their wine is ready, the sources we found were spotty and entirely inconsistent. Although the barrels were cheap: a barrel that the winemaker had paid about $1,000 for, and used only one time, cost us $15 including transportation.

We brought our first small shipment of barrels to Trenton, just enough to fill the test market order for Home Depot, and put Ron to work. Everything went fine—Ron did good work and we fulfilled the order on time. The product blew off the shelves, and of course that meant we would have to do the same thing again, but in a much greater volume. There wasn't really enough space in the Trenton factory to do the work of converting a large number of barrels, and, besides, we didn't really want to ship the barrels from California to Trenton and then ship them back, in some cases, to customers in California. It was obvious that the construction should be done in California, which meant that we would have to go there and find somewhere to do it. As always time was running out. Before long, we would have to ship the now large order (over two thousand barrels) to Home Depot.

I flew out to California to look for a production site. The thing about barrels, after all, is that they're big. They're about five feet tall and four feet in diameter at the widest, so you need a lot of warehouse space if you're dealing with them. The issue very quickly became where to put all the barrels. In talking with one of the vineyards we were getting barrels from, I was asked the question of where we would want all of the barrels shipped to.

"Well, I'll have to get back to you about that," I said. "I'm actually here looking for a place to convert the barrels." They asked what kind of a place I needed, and I said that it didn't have to be very elaborate. We really just needed a big open space where Ron could do the kind of simple carpentry that was necessary.

"We've got a big old barn in the back that we're not using," they said. "Would that be the kind of thing you need?" It was another amazing stroke of luck. Not only was it available, they were willing to lease it to us month-by-month, which we wanted at least until we had a steady sale of composters or rain barrels. I was so relieved that I took a quick look at the barn and told them that we'd take it. Huge problem solved.

But now I had to tell Ron that the operation was moving twenty-five hundred miles west. I flew back to Trenton, trying to figure out how to put it to him. I felt really bad that we had basically offered him a job and now were taking it away from him. When I got to work, I called him into my office and said, "Look, Ron, we're very happy with your work, but we've realized that we just won't be able to make the composters and rain barrels here in Trenton. There just isn't space."

He didn't bat an eye. "Okay," he said. "Where do you want me to go?"

I hadn't expected this. "Well, we have this space in California. . . ."

"Okay," he said. "When do you want me to be there?"

The next day, he packed his family and belongings into a car and drove to California.

As usual, we were under the gun. We had to get that order ready in a hurry. There were a lot of shipments of different sizes going to different places, and the forms from the big retailers are always complicated, so Robin flew out a week before the shipment had to be ready to troubleshoot any difficulties. He called up after he'd been there for a while.

"Tom, did you look at this barn before you leased it?"

Uh-oh, I thought. "Of course I did. I didn't inspect every inch of it. It was just what we needed, where we needed it, and it was available. Is there something wrong?"

"You could say that. It doesn't have any electricity, for one thing. Ron needs electricity to cut the barrels."

"Well, you can rent a generator, right?"

"It doesn't have a bathroom, either."

"You're on a farm in the middle of nowhere, I'm sure as a man you could improvise."

"It doesn't have a floor. There's just dirt."

"Well, yes, but you don't really need a concrete floor for the barrels."

"Tom, the roof leaks. And it's been raining for three days."

Robin finished the order literally up to his knees in muck. I really owe him for that one. He got the order out, on time, and Home Depot had a terrific success with them. The rain barrels especially. They couldn't keep them in the stores. Once again, we had satisfied a need with garbage.

It occurs to me that this would be a good place to clear up a misconception that would be easy to form about our products. Just because we make things out of other people's waste doesn't mean that we don't care about their quality, or their qualities. We still demand that our products be outstanding, not only in their ability to accomplish the job, but also in their appearance and durability. After we fulfilled the first orders for the composters and rain barrels, we noticed that the barrels we were getting from the vineyards weren't always adequate, at least by our standards. Robin began an exhaustive and exhausting search among all of Napa's vineyards to find a place that could give us a steady supply of good barrels and finally was able to partner with Kendall-Jackson, one of the largest wineries in California and also one of the most environmentally conscious. Not all waste is created equal.

There are a number of ways to categorize and classify waste. The two typical ways to look at waste are preconsumer (or postindustrial) and postconsumer. Preconsumer waste is waste that is created before we ever see the product we consume. This waste is almost always a pure stream, unmixed with anything else, and is the by-product of making the things that fill our stores. For example, there's the fabric that was trimmed when the clothes you are wearing right now were made. Or the paper trimmed from the pages that went into making this book. Preconsumer waste is by far the biggest source of waste in the world and is also the easiest to upcycle since it typically comes in large, consistent quantities, the supply of it is reliable, and you don't have to separate out stuff you don't want.

Postconsumer waste is the waste that you and I produce

in our daily lives. It is the Starbucks paper coffee cup that we throw away, or the wrapper from the Mars Bar we just ate, or the plastic foam box our airplane sandwich came in, or even the wrapper that sandwich was wrapped in. Consider every product you touched today, and you'll see just how pervasive the waste problem is. You wake up and go to the bathroom, creating your own special type of waste. Your toothpaste tube, lip balm container, deodorant case, and so forth are all waste once they are empty. Then at breakfast, the liner your cereal came in, the coffee packaging your coffee beans come in, and your energy bar wrapper are all waste. There's nothing you can do with them but put them into your garbage can. This goes on and on until you go to bed and stop doing anything.

Though there is less of it than preconsumer waste, postconsumer waste is a more difficult problem to attack. Mainly because it's composed of a lot of different stuff—different kinds of stuff, in fact. If you want to make something from postconsumer waste—let's say, used razor blades—you would have to go through tons and tons of garbage before you could amass a few hundred pounds of razor blades to make whatever you wanted. For the most part, that is not a profitable venture for any sane businessman.

Today the most common fates for preconsumer waste are a landfill, an incinerator, or resale for the commodity value of the material it comprises. Typically, this means it is sold to a recycler, who then breaks it down into its raw form and sells it on the commodities market. That's what happens to around 30 percent of our plastic, paper, aluminum, and glass waste. Recycling is better than incineration or landfill, but it's not always the most energy-efficient way to deal with waste. No matter how you look at it, breaking down a material takes energy. In most cases it takes less energy to make a product from recycled materials than from new materials—making aluminum cans out of recycled aluminum scrap uses 95 percent less energy than making aluminum cans from bauxite ore, the raw material used to make aluminum. However, there are many exceptions to the recycling-saves-energy rule, notably plastics. The recycling paradigm typically looks at the materials the object is made from and would view a wine barrel as a combination of wood and steel that would need to be separated, broken down, and then reformed. A recycling approach would expend a great deal of energy and turn that rain barrel into steel ore and compost (the wood would be chipped and then composted).

Just as with our first sale to Wal-Mart, the successful upcycling of wine barrels into composters and rain barrels had a momentum of its own. Now we were known not only as an organic plant food company but as a company that had a much broader brand. We had created distinctive products from garbage, and other companies began coming to us, asking us to create something for them. Target came to us and asked us to make a clock out of garbage. We started looking at vinyl records and realized that if you heat them just a bit, you can mold them into any shape you want.

The first step when you find a new waste stream is to look at all the things you can do with it: cut it, melt it, heat it, fuse it. Once you develop a way to manipulate it, a whole new world opens up. That's what we do today, and as a result we make hundreds of unique upcycled products in categories that range from kites to fire logs.

A year after we first began using the wine barrels in our production, we decided to use the other part of the wine waste stream: in an effort to make a corkboard for OfficeMax we created the first mass-produced used-cork corkboard.

It works the other way, too. People started coming to us with ideas. There was a guy in Victoria, a lovely island off the coast of British Columbia, whose grandfather had always made a deer repellent that he mixed together himself and sold locally. Its ingredients were basically all things that you could find around your house, maybe with a trip to the hardware store. Old eggs were a prime component. When he decided to retire from the deer-repellent business he gave it to his grandson, who eventually found us.

Anybody who lives in the Northeast and hears the words "deer repellent" immediately sits up and takes notice. Deer are the biggest pests that home owners face. In fact, in order to test the deer repellent, all we had to do was go to Bill Gillum's home. On any given evening, he's likely to have a couple of dozen deer eating the plants in his backyard. The deer repellent worked beautifully, we packaged it in upcycled bottles, and we had a terrific new product.

My view of waste had completely changed. I was walking around and every time I saw something that we typically consider waste I was looking at it as a commodity, an object, and trying to analyze what valuable features that object had that could be used to make a product. The first step is to identify the valuable aspects of the object beyond its raw materials. The next step is to think about what current products require these characteristics. With this approach, the idea of garbage disappears and you're left with a bunch of readily available commodities with unique characteristics—that are being incredibly mismanaged.

Over time I started to discover another element of waste that could lead to another way to classify it. This has to do with how much people care about the waste that is being produced. For example, every business produces office waste. Because every business produces this form of waste, they feel relatively little ownership or responsibility. Then there is industry-specific waste, such as plastic foam packaging for electronics. Here people only care if everyone in the industry starts to care. Then there are all those candy-bar wrappers and plastic cartons and coffee cups. They have a very unique characteristic: they all have a company's brand on them. Think about a product—Stonyfield Farm Yogurt. Yogurt containers are made of a certain kind of plastic that is not recyclable in today's national recycling infrastructure. So a container of

Stonyfield Farm is bought, eaten, and thrown out. But up until that container is thrown out, it serves as an advertisement for Stonyfield Farm. If it winds up as a piece of litter crushed on the sidewalk, it will serve as a negative advertisement, undoing the millions of dollars of marketing that was invested behind that brand. Stonyfield Farm, like many companies, would pay to avoid negative advertising.

I call this waste stream "branded waste." Companies care about it more than any other waste form, since it has their name plastered on it. Branded waste, whether preconsumer or postconsumer, is a very unique waste stream that has monstrous implications. The full realization of these implications came to fruition when I got a call from my friend Seth Goldman, the CEO of Honest Tea.

CHAPTER 10

Branded Waste and the Launch of Sponsored Waste

I first met Seth Goldman at an *Inc.* magazine panel about encouraging entrepreneurship, but we didn't start talking about juice pouches until a later conference on organic products, one of the many meetings and conferences about green business that I was now being asked to attend on a regular basis. Seth wanted to show that capitalists could be environmentally friendly, too, just as I did. And he makes tea. Not only that, he even bought one of our composters as a birthday present for his wife. (It's what she'd asked for.)

He launched Honest Tea in 1998 out of his kitchen, and it's now the best-selling bottled tea in the natural foods industry. The name, by the way, came from his partner, Barry Nalebuff. When Seth first got the idea, Barry had just returned from India, where he had been analyzing the tea industry for a case study. Among other things, Barry had learned that most of the tea leaves purchased for brewing and bottling by American companies was the lower-quality residue left after the higher-quality tea leaves had separated out. Barry had even come up with a name to describe a bottled tea that was made with real tea leaves—Honest Tea. Seth agreed that it was the perfect name to fit an all-natural brand that would "strive to create healthy and honest relationships with its customers, suppliers and the environment," as their Web site puts it. Five weeks later, he took some of the tea drinks he'd made to Whole Foods and found himself with an order for fifteen thousand bottles. Even though he didn't have a factory. Sounds very familiar to me.

At the organic products conference, Seth brought up a problem that had just come up in his business. He had spent months getting ready to launch Honest Kids, a line of juice drinks for kids that, like the adult drinks, would contain less sugar and no artificial ingredients—a pure organic juice drink for children. However, whereas drinks marketed for adults were sold in recyclable glass and plastic bottles, juice pouches were the only way to really compete for the kid market. Juice pouches are everywhere for kids—4.5 billion of them are produced a year in the United States alone.

And unfortunately all of them end up in landfills. Juice pouches fuse plastic with aluminum in a single material. What people don't realize is that most flexible plastic is not recyclable, and the combination of flexible plastic and metal is a killer. The good part about juice pouches is that they are much lighter and use less material than any other container and therefore add less waste to our world. So Seth wanted to stick with that form of container, but he asked his manufacturer to come up with a juice pouch that would be made of PET, a recyclable form of plastic. Just before I saw him at the conference, he'd been told that Honest Kids juice pouches would be made of PET—except for the bottom, which had to be aluminum and plastic.

This was Seth's problem. If there was any aluminum at all, the pouch couldn't be recycled. His juice pouch would become an example of what William McDonough and Michael

Braungart call a "monstrous hybrid" in their book *Cradle to Cradle*. They point out that we have compounded the difficulties of recycling by putting together materials that, individually, might degrade naturally or be recycled but in combination are totally resistant to either. While aluminum by itself can be recycled easily, and some plastics can be recycled (specifically, the plastic in Seth's juice pouches), when you put the two together, there's nothing you can do but throw it into a landfill. So he asked me if we could come up with a solution to keep all of those used juice pouches from heading for that fate. I realized during that call from Seth that for the first time someone was asking us to solve brand-specific waste. What concerned him was that Honest Kids juice pouches would wind up being litter. Mangled and dirty. Brand-specific waste is important to a company because their logo is plastered all over it. Seth didn't want to see Honest Kids pouches lying on the sidewalk or sitting on top of a landfill. Becoming litter is a blemish on the brand name that a company has spent millions or in some cases billions of dollars to build. Coca-Cola spends billions to make sure that its bottle looks good on the shelf, feels good in your hand, and tastes good when you're drinking it. When that bottle winds up on a sidewalk, it's not a good end. While Seth had not spent that much on Honest Tea, he had certainly worked very hard to associate all his products with a responsible attitude toward the planet. When an Honest Kids pouch became litter—or even part of a landfill—his brand image was diluted.

In other words, companies like Seth's would invest money to solve a branded waste problem.

Of course, Honest Tea bottles could also wind up as litter, but Seth is a practical person. He can't be held responsible for what consumers do after they buy the product. It's sufficient that he has made it possible for the product to be recycled. Having the choice is the critical piece. If a package is recyclable, the onus is on the consumer, not the brand, since the brand has already given the consumer the choice. However, with nonrecyclable waste the only choice is a landfill and the fault is clearly in the brand's court for choosing a nonrecyclable package.

This is the challenge that all nonrecyclable waste producers face—and, frankly, the majority of branded waste is nonrecyclable. From a Starbucks paper coffee cup to the Sara Lee plastic bread bag, to the waxed box or flexible plastic that holds your frozen vegetables and ice cream and yogurt. In actual fact, basically the only things that can be recycled (that is, reduced to their useful components and reused to make something new) are hard plastic bottles, paper, and aluminum cans.

Not long after I started talking to Seth, I got a call from Gary Hirshberg, the CE-Yo of Stonyfield Farm Yogurt, asking me to create a solution for his yogurt cups. Like Seth, Gary had worked hard to find the most environmentally friendly packaging for his yogurt. "When we started Stonyfield," he says, "the question was: Is it possible to create commerce that's part of the solution, not part of the problem. I have discovered that sustainable practices are much more profitable than not." So in 1994, Gary decided to switch from yogurt cups made out of what's called "high-density polyethylene" (HDPE) to cups made out of polypropylene (the #5 plastic, which is rarely recycled). Although HDPE is easier to recycle, the particular type of HDPE used for yogurt cups is not accepted by most recycling programs. Since the #5 cups were 20 percent lighter than the HDPE ones, Gary figured that by using the #5 cups, he was actually generating less waste.

That may seem counterintuitive, so I'll try to make it clearer. Most people probably look at recycling in terms of individual things—that is, it's better to recycle a sixteen-ounce glass bottle than to throw away a sixteen-ounce nonrecyclable plastic bottle. But as we've seen with waste in other contexts, it's not always just about size. People who look at recycling and landfills and such tend to think about waste in terms of its sheer weight. (The reason for this gets into the mechanics and economics of reducing things to their component parts.) And they look at the reality of how many things really are recycled—a rough rule of thumb is that 30 percent of the population is actually going to recycle that glass bottle. So out of every ten sixteen-ounce glass bottles, about seven of them wind up in a landfill—about twenty-eight ounces worth. Only twelve ounces are recycled. So if you can reduce the weight of the bottle by half and make it nonrecyclable, only twenty ounces of waste end up in a landfill, which is a better environmental choice.

Naturally, I was happy to try to find upcycling solutions for Seth and for Gary. Starting with the drink pouch, I first tried to figure out how a pouch could be manipulated to make it useful in a different way. What are the characteristics of a pouch that make it useful? Well, it's superstrong and it's about three by five inches in size. The only challenge is how to attach them together into a fabric in a simple way. That reminded me of something I had heard at a conference I'd attended about a group of Filipino women. I went on the Internet and found them.

PREDA stands for the People's Recovery, Empowerment Development Assistance Foundation and it was founded in 1974 in the Philippines by Fr. Shay Cullen, an Irish Columban missionary, and Merle and Alex Hermoso, a Filipino couple dedicated to helping Filipino youth. The original goal was to help teenagers from broken homes who were trying to forget their problems through substance abuse. The PREDA Foundation was set up to help the children "deal with their family problems and to rehabilitate the parents and restore family unity, respect and love." To do that, PREDA tried to find ways for its people to earn a living.

Beginning in September 2004, PREDA began producing, selling, and shipping items made from juice pouches, which are just as common in the Philippines as in this country. They train those who collect the used juice bags (including many school students who help their schools earn money by collecting juice bags on campus), paying them for their efforts and teaching them about the environment. After the collected containers are cleaned and sanitized, PREDA makes them available to the women (and men) who actually produce these handcrafted items. As of April 2006, PREDA had sold over 46,500 bags worldwide. So juice pouches could be transformed into a material—maybe not what you would call fabric, but something that could be sewn into sheets as long as you liked and could be cut or folded or sewn into any shape you needed.

This seemed to be a perfect model for TerraCycle to use in solving Seth's problem. As usual, none of this occurred to me until a few days before I was supposed to meet with Seth in his Bethesda, Maryland, office and present the idea to him. I contacted PREDA to see if they wanted to become part of this, but they are really focused on helping individual Filipinos, and weren't able to do anything really big. But they were happy to let me take the idea and run with it. So I went to Target and bought a couple hundred Honest Kids juice pouches and brought them back to the office. Everybody drank Honest Kids for a couple of days until we had enough pouches to wash and experiment with.

By that time, I was supposed to meet Seth the next day, June 27, 2007. So I bought a sewing machine at Wal-Mart and spent all night with it, first learning how to sew—the biggest problem was threading the machine and breaking needles. Once I had mastered that, I had to figure out how to put pouches together. If you look at a picture of an Honest Kids pouch, you'll see that it's curved in the middle, where people can grip it. So I had to figure out how to sew the curves of the pouch together. Not to mention designing what the finished product should look like. But I stuck with it, and sometime after midnight I had the first Honest Kids drink-pouch tote bag.

Not many hours later, I got up to drive to Maryland for our meeting with Seth. Two other TerraCycle people, Pierre Wang and Alysia Welch-Chester, were driving down separately, but they got stuck in traffic and were an hour late. On top of that, Seth was in the middle of moving his offices, so the only space that was available for a meeting was a supply closet. None of it mattered. Seth loved the idea, loved the bag, and immediately bought into the whole sponsored waste program. Since the brigade program was still growing at a tremendous rate, we couldn't afford to add a juice-pouch brigade without help. We needed to hire someone new to administer the drink-pouch brigade and the management of the bags as they came in, and Seth offered to support it. With his investment, we could open up six hundred locations to collect the pouches. This was the first time in history that a brand paid to solve their nonrecyclable branded waste problem.

There is something miraculous about that moment to me. With one simple handshake, Honest Kids drink pouches stopped having only one fate—being garbage—and now had two possible outcomes: they could be either thrown out or upcycled—"TerraCycled." Suddenly, those drink pouches were not just garbage; they had value ($0.02 each). Seth's investment, made in order to prevent his pouches from becoming garbage, had made his pouches valuable—to me and to the schools and other organizations who would collect them.

Of course we couldn't start with all six hundred locations, but we prepared to set up one hundred of them around the country as a test. We offered them up on the Web site, and within twenty-four hours, we had filled the list. We had to close the offer temporarily and put names on a waiting list. Which shows that this kind of program really fills a need.

Almost the same thing happened with the yogurt cups. When you look at a waste stream, you want to use it for the value that it already has. The key to upcycling is to use as little energy as possible—a lot of energy has been spent to shape the plastic into a yogurt cup, so the best outcome is if we do as little as possible to change that. The best idea that came to us was planting pots, which also fit nicely into our established selling lines to Home Depot and other home-improvement stores and departments. Gardeners toss about 320 million pounds of plastic every year, and plant pots are a significant part of that total. We showed it to Gary, who loved the idea. Holding up a yogurt plant pot in our meeting, he said, "We're going to make you famous. This is a terrific way to show people that these containers have a long way to go." Gary joined in to sponsor a yogurt brigade a couple of weeks after Seth. The yogurt brigade, like the drink-pouch brigade, was a huge success, which just drove home the fact that there was a tremendous demand to upcycle products—bigger even than I had imagined.

One of the coolest things that happened with the drink-pouch program was the result of something Soyeon suggested. We had gone to the Al Gore Live Earth concert in New York and were impressed at how they had used music to make people more aware of the environment. Why not do that in classical music? She had a concert at Carnegie Hall scheduled for the next February and suggested that we use the Honest Kids drink pouches to create a dress for her to play in that night.

I thought that was an outstanding idea, so we found an environmentally conscious designer, Nina Valenti, and worked with her for the next few months. Soyeon had a few requirements for the dress for performance: no sleeves and straps that sit high up on the shoulder. The biggest problem, as it turned out, was just sitting down in the dress gracefully. It had a lot of different parts, so she had to be able to gather them together and take a seat at the piano without a hitch. She practiced that too. No kidding.

The concert was a huge success, and there was tons of publicity. Darryl Hannah has been a supporter of TerraCycle for a long time, and she generously flew into New York City to introduce Soyeon and the concept behind the dress. Soyeon picked pieces that were classical music's version of recycling and reinventing—composers using themes and motifs from other pieces in new ways. "An Eco-Friendly Pianist Wears Her Heart on Her Sleeveless Dress" was the headline of the half-page spread in the *New York Times.*

As the drink-pouch brigades were gearing up, I started pitching this new material concept to retailers, and the response was even more enthusiastic than I ever expected. Walgreens, Target, ShopKo, Wal-Mart, OfficeMax, Meijer, and a few others all agreed to carry various juice-pouch products—we were ready to go with pencil cases, tote bags, backpacks, homework folders, lunch boxes, and other products. The retailers loved them. They were great, unique products with that Andy Warhol kind of look, but just as important to them was the story of the product. We were offering something that was environmentally better than anything currently on the market, and the raw material (the juice pouches) had been collected most likely by a child in a school or a member of a church or a charity somewhere in America. And those organizations had received two cents per pouch as a donation. As you can imagine, they couldn't get enough. That spring was an amazing time for the bottle brigades. After articles in *NEA Today* and *Guideposts* in April 2007, the number of locations collecting bottles shot up from fifteen hundred to four thousand in just a few months. The Honest Tea juice-pouch brigades and the Stonyfield Farm Yogurt brigades were also receiving an enormous amount of publicity.

After a sales meeting with one of America's biggest retailers, I called up Robin and said, "The good news is that Walgreens just gave us a huge new order for the juice-pouch pencil cases."

"Fabulous. But what's the bad news?"

"Well, I've done a rough calculation on how many juice pouches we'll need to make the order."

"Yeah, and . . . ?"

"I figure it will be about ten million juice pouches. And we'll need to start manufacturing in about two weeks."

The big problem was that there weren't enough drink

pouches coming in from the brigade. That wasn't a surprise; we knew the brigades would build slowly because they always do. But we also hadn't expected the size of the response from the retailers. So Robin went on the Internet, and after an all-night search, he found a company called Encorp in Vancouver. It was actually an arm of the government of British Columbia, which had mandated that juice pouches in schools have a deposit on them. This meant that lots of people were collecting them in BC to get the deposit back (which shows what a little economic incentive can do). They had started the Canadian equivalent of a juice-pouch brigade, but the catch was that they didn't have a good solution for reusing them. They couldn't be dumped in a landfill, so until they found a solution, they had to warehouse them.

But "warehouse" isn't the right word, because what they'd done was to put the juice pouches through a baler, which just squashes them into a highly compressed cube. So they wound up with hundreds of three-by-three-by-three-foot blocks of juice pouches, each of which weighed maybe half a ton. They didn't wash them, they didn't take the straws out, they didn't even take them out of the plastic bags they were collected in. Then, since there wasn't anybody who could recycle them, the juice-pouch cubes were being stored in trailers parked in a field in British Columbia. And this had been going on for a couple of years.

So Robin called up someone at Encorp and asked, "Do you have any juice pouches?"

He kind of chuckled and said, "Yeah."

"Well, do you have any idea how many you might have?"

"Oh, I'd say . . . I guess about twenty million."

That was the right number. Robin was beginning to get excited. "Do you mind if I ask what you're doing with them?"

"We're storing them."

Then Robin asked the money question: "Can I have them?"

"I don't know if I can give them to you." Oh yeah, Robin

thought, it's the government. "I'll have to talk to people here. Why don't you send us some information about your company so that we can talk it over here?"

It took Robin about a split second to shoot off a letter about TerraCycle and the unique way we upcycle waste, and how we would use the pouches to make great pencil cases and backpacks and lots of other things for kids. No response. Robin waited a day and called again. Somebody important was on holiday. He'd be back in three weeks. Robin found someone else to talk to and emphasized that we really needed the pouches, and if we didn't get them soon, we would have to go somewhere else.

Finally, one guy said, "We're thinking about it."

That was enough for Robin. He bought an airline ticket and flew to Vancouver to meet with the Encorp official. We needed to see the pouches and see firsthand whether we could use them. The first thing Robin did was to ask to see the bales. So someone went to a trailer with a forklift—in the pouring rain, typical BC weather—and hauled over a hunk of massed juice pouches that was drenched and leaking, and it stunk because the juice had been fermenting there for months or years. The Encorp guy looked at Robin as if to say, "There's no way in the world you want this stuff, is there?" He bent down to the dripping square block of juice pouches in front of Robin, yanked on one of the plastic bag handles until about twenty or thirty pouches came flying out. After looking at them closely and realizing there was no other choice, Robin asked if he could get them all.

Everything was falling into place until Encorp brought up the last, and biggest, problem. Almost all the drink pouches—both from the brigades and the ones that Encorp had collected—were Capri Sun and Kool-Aid brand. Both of those brands are owned by Kraft Foods, the biggest food company in America. Encorp would not release the pouches to us unless they had assurance that Kraft was on board with TerraCycle reusing their pouches. Since we had just resolved the lawsuit with Scotts Miracle-Gro, going up against Kraft Foods was scary.

At this point I had all the purchase orders from the stores in hand, so there was no backing out.

I called Kraft.

CHAPTER 11

Sponsored Waste Takes Off

Both Seth and Gary were as much concerned about the edu-cational aspect of upcycling as they were about the commercial aspects. They didn't want their brands tarnished, but they are also seriously concerned about the environment and about being environmentally responsible businessmen. Both of them talked about the educational opportunity that "TerraCycling" would provide. But what about Kraft Foods? Would a corporate giant like Kraft be willing to have their logo on a TerraCycle pencil case? I had no idea.

What I did know is that if they were going to oppose the project, I had a serious problem on my hands. If they simply declined to take part, Encorp wouldn't allow us to bring down the juice boxes that they had been stockpiling.

The question of intellectual property rights concerning waste is tricky. Obviously, all these brands have various levels of intellectual property protected. For example, no one can come along and use the built-up power of the brand name, its attributes or look—in other words, their trade dress—to sell their own product. Take a Coke bottle, for instance. People are prohibited from using a bottle shaped like a Coke bottle to sell their own drink, since the customers might be confused as to who made the product. Was it made by Coke or someone else? However, that shape is not protected if you fill it with something else—like worm poop, for instance. Coke can only sue you if they can show that you are leveraging that particular shape to sell your product. For example, if we said "buy worm poop in Coke bottles" and didn't use any other brand's bottles. So if I take all kinds of bottles and put liquid worm poop in them, and it's very clear that the shape of the bottle itself is not what I'm using to sell my poop, then they can't sue successfully. But the laws, and the interpretations of the laws, are still very vague when it comes to waste. It's possible that Capri Sun doesn't own the shape and design of their juice pouch if it is sewn together with other brands of juice and made into a tote bag.

Either way, I had no choice. The overwhelming number of Capri Sun and Kool-Aid pouches that were coming in from the brigade and Encorp meant that I would be using these two brands almost exclusively. I thought that branded waste was a powerful new tool in TerraCycle's arsenal, and at the same time it addressed an important part of the planet's environmental worries.

I decided that I would go to Kraft and at least get a definite answer from them one way or the other as to whether we could use Capri Sun and Kool-Aid juice pouches. Once I had that yes or no, I would figure out what to do next.

But who was I supposed to talk to? It didn't feel appropriate to write to the CEO directly, and the last thing I wanted to do was to call up their legal department.

The first surprise was that Kraft had a vice president in charge of "sustainability." So I looked at their sustainability report, which is available on their Web site, to find out his name and asked him to connect me with the right person in his department to talk to about Capri Sun and Kool-Aid. He directed me to Vinay Sharma, who was the brand manager for Capri Sun. I sent him an e-mail explaining that TerraCycle manufactures eco-friendly, affordable products that are made from and packaged in waste. I gave him some examples and described the brigades and how children (of all ages) were involved with the programs and how educational it could be for them.

All I told him about the juice pouches was that we were in the midst of launching a line of pencil cases and tote bags made from various sewn-together drink pouches to be sold by major retailers the following spring, and that the idea had already generated the promise of very good publicity in several major magazines. I said I'd like to meet with him to describe the program in more detail. Luckily, *20/20* was going to broadcast a feature on TerraCycle that very Friday.

Within a day or so, he responded:

> Thanks for reaching out to me. Would love to meet up in person. I have read about TerraCycle and am very intrigued by what you guys do. In addition to the new line of bags and pencil cases, I'd love to talk to you about the pouch brigade and how (or if) we can get involved. Environmental consciousness is becoming top of mind for even the younger consumers today, and Capri Sun needs to be part of the trend.

That sounded promising, but it was too soon to start celebrating. Early in November 2007, Albe Zakes and I went up to see Vinay for the first time in his office in Tarrytown, New York. I was incredibly nervous, since they had the power to shut down the program.

You couldn't find a place more different from TerraCycle's Trenton factory than Kraft's Tarrytown offices. "One day TerraCycle will have a campus like this," I told Albe. There was a security gate at the main entrance, and then we got lost trying to find Vinay's building. So we had to check in with a second security guard, who had to call our names in. I don't imagine there has ever been any stray gunfire anywhere in those offices, unlike our Trenton office.

Needless to say, we were completely out of place. Even the receptionist who handed us our visitor's passes looked at us funny. We were dressed pretty much as usual, in jeans and T-shirts, and of course we were carrying tote bags and backpacks and pencil cases that we'd made up with Capri Sun juice pouches (maybe it was the backpacks that caught her eye).

When we got to Vinay's office, he couldn't have been more welcoming. The first thing he said to us was, "Okay, we're in. How shall we make this work?" That was the real revelation. He saw what we were offering as a way to add distinction to his brand, and he didn't mind at all that Capri Sun would be the first mega-brand to be TerraCycled. I quickly saw, not only that we would be able to work out a licensing agreement that would allow TerraCycle to use the Capri Sun and Kool-Aid pouches, but that he was expecting to talk about becoming a sponsor.

It that brief conversation we had taken a huge step forward. We walked out of the meeting with a licensing agreement and a handshake that we would work together on a sponsorship agreement. On February 6, 2008, we signed a contract that would scale up the drink-pouch brigade from the six hundred locations it involved at the time to five thousand.

This was an epic moment, a watershed in upcycling. Honest Kids represented perhaps one-tenth of 1 percent of the drink-pouch market. Capri Sun and Kool-Aid together represented well over 90 percent. Almost 80 percent of all juice pouches are consumed in schools, so pouches are ideal not only from the standpoint of the school raising funds but also in terms of the educational value of upcycling versus trashing the pouch. By working out this agreement with Capri Sun we were able to create a program that essentially locked up the entire drink-pouch market, created a scalable national upcycling infrastructure, and could create real, massive change. No longer would all 4.5 billion drink pouches wind up in landfills every year. As of February 2008, there was a choice that anyone in America could be a part of.

All this was exactly what large companies like Kraft were looking for. The concern about climate change that was put in sharp focus by *An Inconvenient Truth* was beginning to affect all large corporations. Kraft was not unusual in having formed a sustainability division. What the companies were discovering was that being environmentally conscious could reduce their costs and increase their profitability.

Capri Sun's support was just the tip of the iceberg. Now that we had a program with them, other Kraft brands started showing interest. We started getting calls from Oreo, Chips Ahoy! and Balance Bar to see if we could help them out.

While we were launching the program with Kraft, we were approached by Clif Bar, a company that was founded by Gary Erickson—he has a story that is a lot like Seth's. A serious cyclist and also the owner of a bakery in Berkeley, California, he didn't like any of the energy bars that were available. So in 1992, he started making his own energy bar—the Clif Bar, named after his father—and quickly became one of the fastest-growing companies in the United States. In 2000, Gary turned down a $120 million offer for the company. Like Honest Tea, environmental awareness is a key principle in his business, and Clif Bar came to us to see if we could upcycle Clif Bar wrappers. Since these wrappers are part aluminum, like juice pouches, they are also not recyclable and a fantastic candidate for upcycling. Within a month, the Clif Bar energy bar wrapper brigade was launched.

We were already making materials out of wrappers when we were introduced to the people at Kraft's Balance Bar, Oreo, Chips Ahoy! and South Beach Diet Bar. Like the juice pouches, Oreo and Chips Ahoy! cookie package wrappers are not recyclable, but for a different reason. They are composed of several super-thin layers of different kinds of plastics, each of which provides a different advantage in terms of protecting the cookies from moisture, air, and sunlight, keeping them fresh whenever you open that package and making it easy to print nice graphics on them.

But in terms of recycling, those plastics are a problem. For one thing, recycling businesses are often paid by the ton, and it takes an awful lot of cookie package wrappers to make up a ton. But because these different plastics melt at different temperatures and react differently from each other in various other ways, it is difficult and expensive to separate those fine layers for recycling. They are yet another kind of synthetic hybrid, a product that won't die naturally. A lighter wrapper is "environmentally beneficial because it uses less material and less energy per package," says David Cornell, the technical director of the Association of Postconsumer Plastic Recyclers in Washington, D.C. "This is all fine and dandy until the package gets to the end of its life." What we knew was that the end of its life as a package is only the beginning of its life as a pencil pouch or the like. Once again, TerraCycling filled a need that was going unanswered. The brand managers were extremely excited to see what we could do for them, and several of them immediately began work launching brigades. Within a couple of months, we had launched the cookie wrapper brigade with sponsorship from Oreo, Chips Ahoy! and Nabisco (the four largest cookie brands in America). Balance Bar and South Beach Diet Bar became sponsors alongside Clif Bar on the energy bar wrapper brigade.

This landslide embracement at Kraft was exactly the opposite of what I thought would happen, but it's an indication of just how enormous the potential of sponsored waste is. Kraft is the biggest food company in America, with over $30 billion in sales per year. Different flavors of Oreos and Chips Ahoy! are the four largest-selling cookie brands in America and sell hundreds of millions of packages per year. Our partnership with Kraft took the little idea that we had pioneered with Honest Tea, Stonyfield Farm, and Clif Bar and expanded it to mega scale.

There is an irony in this. Gary Hirshberg came up with the idea of Stonyfield Farm because he took a tour of a Kraft-sponsored pavilion on the future of food at Disney World's Epcot Center in Florida. At the time he was head of a nonprofit organization called the New Alchemy Institute, which studied how to produce food and energy with no fossil fuels. In 1982 (the year I was born), he went to visit his mother, who was then the senior buyer at Epcot. He happened to visit when Kraft was running a pavilion that offered their view of how foods would be produced in the future, and he found their ideas shocking: "But the big shocker of that day was not the incredible widespread use of fossil fuels and CO_2 emissions and so on, it was the fact that for the twenty-five thousand people who visited my institute every year, that many people visited them every day." He realized that if he was going to have a real impact on the environment, he would have to be as big as Kraft.

As you look at any waste material, like Oreo wrappers, you need to focus on what basic materials you can make from it. For example, Oreo wrappers can be fused into a fabric and woven, which makes it possible to make placemats, coasters, tablecloths, wrapping paper, designer bags, reusable bags, shower curtains, umbrellas, spiral notebooks, pencil cases, three-ring binders, messenger bags, kids' backpacks . . . fundamentally anything. And that's just the beginning. To put it into perspective, all of these TerraCycle products were in widespread big-box distribution before the end of 2008 (almost one year from the date the cookie wrapper brigade was launched)!

But the biggest benefit of all is the way Kraft can get TerraCycle's message out to the world—and the way that TerraCycle can create a landmark sustainability solution for Kraft. Since TerraCycle has become a major part of Kraft's sustainability program, the brands have embraced us in more ways than just helping to fund the collection program. Capri Sun launched a thirty-second commercial on Cartoon Network in late 2008, highlighting the TerraCycle drink-pouch brigade and the products that TerraCycle makes from the pouches. From full-page advertisements in national magazines to advertising on the Web, the marketing of these programs by Kraft allowed megascale to be realized. To me the biggest win of all was that in late 2008 each Chips Ahoy! package and all Capri Sun boxes started carrying a description of the TerraCycle program—over half a billion packages highlighting an upcycling solution, as recycling is highlighted on bottles.

The statement read: "Chips Ahoy! is partnering with TerraCycle to collect used cookie wrappers and turn them into cool eco-friendly products like backpacks, pencil cases and totes. This helps keep them out of landfills and has a positive impact on the environment."

On July 1, 2008, we officially launched the program in the media with a leadoff article in the *Wall Street Journal* that began:

> Each year, billions of food and drink wrappers encasing popular brands end up in landfills because their multilayered materials—which keep products fresh—are tricky and expensive to break down and recycle. This waste has presented a challenge for manufacturers eager to reduce their environmental impact and buff reputations among eco-conscious consumers.
>
> But that's changing due to an unusual alliance between a growing number of food and beverage bigwigs—including Kraft Foods Inc., Kellogg Co., Clif Bar & Co. and Coca-Cola Co.—and a tiny company in Trenton, N.J., named TerraCycle Inc.
>
> "What TerraCycle has done so well is they've created products that aren't boring," says Ryan Vero, chief merchandising officer at OfficeMax, which stocks TerraCycle's Capri Sun and Kool-Aid binders and pencil pouches and has ordered computer bags for the fall. "That's cool for back to school. We even have executives carrying them around this building."

Since that article ran, there has been a new article about the program almost every day.

Kraft joining created major credibility and allowed this program to be embraced by other mega-brands. Shortly after we announced our partnership with Kraft we got calls from companies that include P&G, General Mills, Nestle Purina, Nike, Disney, Warner Bros., Sara Lee, Frito-Lay, and many others about launching similar mega-upcycling programs.

What's amazing in what happened here is the potential of where this can go. Today there are thousands of recycling centers across America, taking in plastic, paper, and metal products. While this is a terrific success story from one point of view, these centers also use lots of energy to reduce this waste back into its basic elements. Then they sell these remainders to companies that then typically use a bunch of energy to turn them into inferior products (versus the quality of using virgin materials). For example, a plastic bottle can contain at most 30 percent recycled plastic or it becomes unstable. To take another example, it's not really possible to make a high-quality piece of paper from 100 percent recycled paper. Unlike metals and glass, both plastics and papers degrade through the recycling process.

Recycling is great, but it is not a true cradle-to-cradle process—that is, it's not about renewing products and works only with a limited number of polymers. McDonough and Braungart describe the lives of common products as following a "cradle-to-grave" design. "Resources are extracted, shaped into products, sold, and eventually disposed of in a 'grave' of some kind, usually an incinerator or a landfill." In contrast, a tree extracts resources from the ground, grows into a huge thing, but when it dies, it returns all the resources it extracted back to where they came from (except for sunlight)—it's the perfect example of cradle-to-cradle design. More importantly, the amount of nonrecyclable branded waste out there is estimated at more than five times the recyclable waste out there.

TerraCycling creates new products from what was considered waste. By the time this book is published, we will have over thirty thousand micro-upcycling locations (brigades—feel free to sign up your group at www.terracycle.net) across America, with an average participation of 169 people. That's millions of Americans already participating in our programs. Over the past year, over 50 million used drink pouches have been upcycled by TerraCycle (collected through the brigade and other acquisitions). Our goal is that by the end of 2011 we will have over two hundred thousand locations across America participating. The crazy part is that this is a conceivable achievement, since the biggest brands in America are seriously focused and committing resources to make this happen. Landmark brands are embracing the program and putting the TerraCycling message on their packaging. This is resulting in billions upon billions of impressions about the brigade programs each year.

The modern recycling infrastructure gave a choice to the American consumer to be able to do something other than throw out glass, plastic, and paper. Over time, through the growing national TerraCycle infrastructure, the American consumer is being given a choice to upcycle an ever-growing list of nonrecyclable waste.

The potential of this system is huge and the implementation daunting, but with the support of the world's biggest brands and the world's biggest retailers, it is one that is entirely realistic and, moreover, actually being implemented on the largest of scales.

The impact on the environment is significant. Not only are we keeping hundreds of tons of nonrecyclable materials from ending up in landfills, we are eliminating the need for that same quantity of new nonrecyclable materials from ever being produced. And best part is that you can even return the upcycled products we make into the collection program when you are done with it; we'll give multiple credits to the brigade's charity (depending on the number of upcycled materials in the product) and the cycle continues.

CHAPTER 12

Upcycled Marketing

Just as the sponsored waste programs were gearing up, I was asked to give a keynote to Target's executive team, during the company's design week. Design has always been important to Target—both the products and the design of the store itself, and every year they focus on it for a week. In 2008, I spoke there about sustainable design—essentially telling them all the things I had learned up to that point about waste and its many uses. I made the point that we at TerraCycle believed we could take any substantial waste stream and turn it into usable, useful products.

Afterward, a few of the Target folks took me out to dinner, and at one point I asked Sally Mueller, a Target marketing executive, "Sally, what waste problem can we solve for you?" She laughed and said, "Plastic bags. You can solve our plastic bag problem." The reason she laughed is because plastic bags are so common, so universal, and are such an enormous environmental problem that it seemed inconceivable to her that anyone could really do very much about it.

It's difficult, in fact, to get a handle on how many plastic bags there are in the world, or what happens to them. It's also amazing how recently they have become a problem. The basic plastic shopping bag was only created in the late 1970s by a man named Gordon Dancy. (Before his death, he began a business dedicated to recycling plastic.) Thirty years later, the world uses somewhere between 500 billion and 1 trillion bags each year (the number is hard to pin down precisely). The United States alone uses nearly 400 billion bags and wraps of all kinds every year. That's more than a thousand bags per year for every man, woman, and child in the country. According to the *Wall Street Journal,* Americans use 100 billion plastic shopping bags alone yearly, which consumes 12 million barrels of oil and costs retailers $4 billion—which, of course, they pass along to us.

What's wrong with a plastic bag? After all, it's very light, and as we've seen with Honest Tea and Stonyfield Farm, weight is an important factor in computing your waste footprint. In addition, plastic is actually more environmentally friendly (or less environmentally evil) than paper—making a paper grocery store bag demands four times the energy it takes to make a plastic one, generates much more pollution in its manufacture, and requires ten times as much energy to recycle.

When it's recycled, that is. But that, unfortunately, is not very often. Estimates vary, but most say that the percentage of plastic bags that are recycled is in the single digits. In part, that's because of the nature of the stuff, and in part because the economics of recycling lightweight plastic just aren't there. It costs $4,000 to recycle a ton of plastic bags, but the market value of that ton is only $32. So why are grocery stores setting up bins for you to recycle your plastic bag? Well, probably they really aren't. Most of them are either taken to a landfill or shipped to a third world country where the laws about incinerating them are more lax.

But the worst part is that plastic bags can't be broken down by biological processes, which is the fastest way to break something down without creating pollutants. I mean, you've never seen a rotting plastic bag, have you? That's because light is the main way that plastic bags degrade, and it works very slowly on plastic bags. So they blow around our streets and rivers and oceans almost forever. They are eaten by sea turtles, who think they are jellyfish. And even when they start to degrade, they still don't disappear. They just break up into smaller and smaller bits over a period as long as one thousand years. These bits are great at soaking up some kinds of toxic chemicals and are then ingested by fish—and therefore probably by us, from time to time. They are clogging drains in India and plugging up the stomachs of whales.

The situation is so serious that governments are getting into the act. In 2002, Ireland instituted an extremely successful plastic bag consumption tax, PlasTax. Consumers paid an extra fifteen cents per bag that they took from the store. Not only did the tax reduce consumption by 90 percent, it also brought in almost $10 million that was used to set up a fund for environmental projects. Plastic bags are now banned in San Francisco and other places around the world. In November 2008, Mayor Bloomberg of New York City proposed a penalty on all plastic bags in the city.

But it seems unlikely that more taxes will make much headway in the United States anytime soon, and local bans will remain just that, local. Ireland became a success story because its people enthusiastically accepted the idea—it became a social black mark to be seen carrying a disposable plastic bag. Unlike Ireland, America is a huge country, with people of all ages, backgrounds, and interests. While there's concern about the environment now, still only about a third of the population is willing to take action to do something about it.

Reusable bags are the solution most people think of first. While they are an improvement, you have to remember that everything has to come from some raw material. It takes energy to make the biodegradable plastic or fiber used to make the bag—and as they degrade, they will contribute pollutants to the environment. Most are currently made from nonwoven polypropylene, which is not an eco-friendly material. Therefore, the typical reusable bag is eco-friendly only in its function—that it replaces a plastic bag—but, frankly, it is just a heavy-duty plastic bag that you can reuse, with all the negative consequences that flow when its usable life comes to an end.

So that was the challenge from Target—although really it was more of a joking aside in Sally's mind. She wasn't really expecting me to give her an answer. To me the scale of the problem alone was exciting because here was an enormous amount of raw material that wouldn't be hard to find.

If we could create a durable reusable bag out of plastic bags, then we would offer a replacement for disposable bags, divert millions of plastic bags from landfills, oceans, and animals, and reduce pollution—because the bag should theoretically last as long as the plastic it's made from. Maybe not forever, but for an awfully long time. As long as I wasn't using very much energy to re-form the bags, it would be the perfect solution.

So that was the key. How do you make a disposable plastic bag into something that would be strong but also could be sewn together to make a bag? We had had great success sewing together the juice pouches, so my first thought was whether we could turn these bags into a material. But unlike the juice pouches, a single bag was way too flimsy to be sewn on its own.

That made me wonder if you could fuse the bags in a reasonably simple way that wouldn't require much energy. So I looked around on the Internet and, lo and behold, there were instructions. Do it yourself and see—just search for "fuse plastic bags." A site called etsy.com, which is a group of people who are dedicated to making things by hand and telling people how to make things by hand, had a video of how to fuse plastic bags with an ordinary household iron. You flatten out the bags, put them between some wax paper so that the plastic doesn't melt onto your iron, and heat them about fifteen seconds on each side. You have to have relatively clean bags, and if they are printed, you have to turn them inside out. You wind up with a very high-quality material that you can use to make all sorts of things, just like the material we created from juice pouches but lighter and more flexible.

So naturally I got an iron—this time from Target—and collected some plastic bags and took them into the TerraCycle office. Albe and I played around with the design for a while, and then I asked Pierre Wang, who had also worked on Honest Tea and Stonyfield Farm, to take over the project. Pierre came to TerraCycle from Seattle, and he had flown three thousand miles to interview for a job we posted on Craigslist in 2007. He was happy to take the lead on the plastic bag fabric. The ironing process isn't really hard to do, but there is a learning curve, and in Pierre's case the learning curve was paid for by our conference table. It was the only place that had enough room, and the finish on the conference table didn't survive. But after all, the table itself had once been garbage. We tried different thicknesses of plastic bags and wound up with eight layers for the bottom and two layers on the side. So fundamentally, we had solved Sally's problem, in about a week.

The last part of the development was to figure out how to mass-produce the fusing process. We clearly couldn't just buy a lot of irons and do it ourselves. Eventually, we were able to construct a machine that looks a little like the pants presser that dry cleaners use. Once you've identified the material, developing the product is the easy part. The hard part is figuring out how to use the garbage. Once you've figured out how to do that, a thousand products suddenly become an option.

Sally was astonished and delighted. Soon afterward, Target put in a huge order for what was later called a "reTote." They began to ship us the bags they had been collecting from the California stores (where bags are collected by law in stores that carry groceries, including Target). This consisted of a truckload of bags a week (roughly a quarter of a million bags in each truck). By this time, we had simply run out of space in the New York Avenue factory. We were making so many products—probably thirty at that point. It was clear to me that we would be making many more soon. So we found a huge empty space in another part of Trenton—nearly a block long, 250,000 square feet, that we could buy for next to nothing, as these things go.

Just about this time, still early in 2008, *Newsweek* invited me to a meeting to decide on the content for their Earth Day issue for April. They had invited a lot of people in the environmental world, from both nonprofits and business. Seth Goldman and Gary Hirshberg were there, for instance.

What I thought was incredibly funny was that every magazine publishes a green issue (from *Vanity Fair* to *Time* to *Vogue*) for Earth Day. Inevitably, they all wind up writing more or less about the same things. So I tried to think of something that would be truly different. Like everything else about TerraCycle, it should have something to do with using waste in a different way, and I also thought it was important that readers of the magazine actually do something, rather than just reading about something—the way the bottle brigades bring kids into the process, which makes them more interested in the results.

Although the technology has improved a great deal in recent years, so that glossy magazines are recycled more often, it's still rare that the cover of a glossy magazine, with its heavy inks, is recycled. So I focused on doing something with the cover. Typically, TerraCycling would involve setting up a site where people could turn in their old magazine covers so that they could be reused.

What if the cover of the magazine itself became the mailer? The outside, of course, would be editorial—a big photo and headlines. But the inside could have TerraCycle's address. I picked up a napkin and doodled about how someone could detach the magazine cover, refold it, and tape three sides to make an envelope. Then you could fill it with whatever you wanted to send to TerraCycle, tape it closed, stamp it, and put it in the mailbox. Instantly, the magazine cover becomes a recycling bin.

Since the inside cover is prime advertising real estate for any magazine, the best course seemed to be to find someone to sponsor it. We would focus on upcycling the product of whoever we could find to sponsor the advertisement. It would be the world's first time a magazine advertisement had ever been upcycled.

I suggested the idea at the meeting and the *Newsweek* people said, "Wow! We think it's great!" I had a number of people in mind and actually pitched it to some of them. But it happened that I was in Minnesota a couple of days later, talking to Target. I saw Sally in one of the halls and asked her if Target would be interested, and she said instantly, "We're in." Target ultimately bought the entire cover.

After Target said yes, we did some testing and wound up figuring that it would take a person about an hour to actually respond. That is, the person would have to remove the ad, do the mechanics of making the envelope, find some bags to put in it, and take it to the post office. And after all, *Newsweek* is a weekly, so we could depend on the push not lasting much beyond the week that the issue was on the stands plus the week after, when the issue had become old and readers would be willing to tear it apart. Based on that, they somehow estimated that we would receive maybe five thousand "cover envelopes" back.

It was a thrill to pick up that copy of *Newsweek,* just months after we were given the plastic bag challenge by Sally.

The first week, we received three thousand bags, well beyond our expectations, but that was nothing compared to what came the next week. Thank God the post office accepted these folded magazine covers in the mail! We inundated the Trenton post office. By the fourth week, we had received more than forty thousand magazine covers—they sent us trucks filled with *Newsweeks*. The amazing thing was that 99.9 percent of the bags received were Target bags. We had to bring people in and train them about how to fuse the bags—and which ones to use. People had left all kinds of things in the bags—receipts, coins, chewing gum, and some things that I don't even want to mention. We had sixty people in Trenton fusing 24/7. It was nuts, but we pulled off the order in the end and shipped over forty thousand reTotes. Since each reTote was composed of twenty plastic bags, that opening order alone saved 800,000 plastic bags.

The program was written about everywhere and has become a model for other kinds of advertising and promotion. And not just because of its environmentally friendly nature. Consider that most people either flip past the advertisement on the inside cover or look at it for maybe five or ten seconds. In this case, forty thousand people spent an hour using the advertisement, and certainly hundreds of thousands more took time to read it and find out what it was all about. Target thought it was so successful that they decided to repeat it only months after in *People* magazine. As you can see, the cover of this book is part of a similar program. Take it off and send us your waste!

The advertisement became an upcycling event and it created one of the best returns on investment for any magazine advertisement. It is a prototype for eco-capitalist marketing, which looks beyond the traditional forms of advertising and promotion to find ways of bringing the consumer into the marketing process.

One of the unusual things about TerraCycle throughout its brief history is how little money we have spent on marketing and advertising. In fact, we have never spent anything on advertising at all! While fulfilling an essential role in collecting packaging for upcycling, the brigades have created waves of local publicity and goodwill across America.

Imagine seeing an article about a program that your son or daughter or niece or nephew was actually participating in.

Then when you saw the product they helped build, in Home Depot or Target, you already had a personal connection to it. And if you were one of the kids who collected a bottle or a juice pouch or a Target bag, you would be especially excited to see a pencil case that it might have been made from. If you were someone who had sent in a Target bag after the *Newsweek* ad, you might be that much more likely to buy a reTote when you see it at Target.

Sponsored waste was our next big breakthrough from a marketing standpoint. By having the TerraCycle brand on billions of products, in conjunction with mega-brands (such as Oreo), which heavily promote their sponsorship (for example, through the *Newsweek* cover advertisement), TerraCycle will become the symbol for upcycling waste.

Traditional advertising is passive, and as the number of print or television ads becomes astronomical, each individual advertisement loses its effectiveness. Upcycled marketing campaigns not only bring special attention to the advertiser, but also create the most powerful experiential, user-generated advertising vehicles.

In truth, I've not found anything (other than toxics) that can't be upcycled and potentially become an economic success—even advertising!

CHAPTER 13

Eco-Capitalist Art and Society

Waste doesn't only exist as a physical object, like that Starbucks coffee cup you may have just thrown out while reading. Waste exists in habits, in processes, in practices, and in ideas. Take, for example, the idea of graffiti. Just type the word "graffiti" into Google's news search and you'll see exactly what I mean. Here is what I got when I recently typed it in:

- Two teens arrested on graffiti charges
- Victim killed for making graffiti
- Graffiti costs Surrey School District nearly $900,000
- County targets parents in graffiti fight
- La Quinta teen arrested on suspicion of $2,000 in graffiti damages

As a society, we spend millions of dollars every year trying to get rid of the idea of graffiti. We spend millions of dollars painting over graffiti on buildings, subway cars, and underpasses. So like the coffee cup you may have just thrown out, we pay money to get rid of it. It is another example of a negative-value commodity. However, in this case it is a negative-value idea, a negative-value form of art.

The problem is that these "artists" can't find a place to paint because no one wants their art on their walls and they can't afford canvases or similar materials. The only places they find to paint are public walls, underpasses, and the like—all illegal spaces. When they do, their art is scoured away, costing local taxpayers millions. The irony in this is that I know a handful of friends in the art-centric neighborhood of SoHo in New York who have spent tens of thousands of dollars to have one of these same artists paint a wall in their pad. In the late seventies, the artists Jean-Michel Basquiat and Keith Haring became celebrated in the art world for their graffiti art, and hence their work became extremely valuable.

Actually, garbage has been part of art for at least a hundred years, ever since Marcel Duchamp used a urinal as a piece of sculpture. Picasso and other cubists incorporated old newspapers in their art, and Robert Rauschenberg used an old quilt and a stuffed goat, among other things, in his sculptures. The Watts Towers in Los Angeles, constructed by Simon Rodia largely from waste, including scrap metal, old bed frames, soda bottles, and milk of magnesia containers, are among the greatest works of folk art in America. Still, we spend millions of dollars to clean graffiti off transportation and buildings and to pay law enforcement to capture graffiti artists. People are arrested daily for pursuing their art form. Of course people cannot be allowed to paint wherever they want—I personally would prefer not having graffiti on my home—but I realized that graffiti was another form of waste that could be turned into an asset.

TerraCycle's graffiti tradition began when we moved into our Trenton factory and invited Leon Rainbow and his friends to paint our walls. They were all pumped by the opportunity to take all the time they wanted—and not have to worry about the cops showing up. Within a month the entire factory was painted. The interest became so massive that the factory turned into a chameleon—as I mentioned, every month the entire factory is entirely repainted. Whether you like the art or not, there is something Buddhist about the mentality of these artists. Somewhat like a musician, they spend hours creating a piece that will not last for more than a week or two. It reminds me of how Buddhist monks spend countless hours creating sand mandalas that, upon completion, they destroy. The irony in all of this is that because graffiti art is waste, as we would define it, instead of paying thousands like my friends in SoHo to have their walls painted, I was doing them a favor by providing the walls without the threat of prosecution.

As the graffiti element at TerraCycle got bigger and bigger we decided to create graffiti jams. We would paint the entire factory black and then during a one-day festival the factory would be repainted with fresh new art. Hundreds of graffiti artists now come to participate. Typically, we have corporate sponsors, DJs, a table where kids can paint, as well as jugglers and other kinds of performers. It's a way for the community to see that the graffiti artists are not just vandals out to deface public places. The funny thing in this is that all TerraCycle did was put the graffiti artists in a different context and suddenly everyone was very positive about it. And the publicity we and they received was terrific, completely the opposite of the negative stories usually written about graffiti. If you go to YouTube and search "TerraCycle Graffiti Jam," you can see clips from several of our annual graffiti weekends.

So in true TerraCycle fashion, we decided to take this form of waste into the world's biggest retailers. Like so many of the other waste streams we have discovered and commercialized, graffiti can be used in all sorts of ways and applied to all sorts of products. As we were playing around with the idea of commercializing graffiti, we were also thinking about what we could do with another new waste stream we'd recently discovered—the plastic components of computers, audio, video, and other electronic products—which we call "e-waste." The problem is that these products are almost impossible to recycle because they contain all sorts of mixed plastics and recycling typically requires that the plastic be one form only.

However, it's obvious that these kinds of electronic products are multiplying at an astonishing rate and most people are unaware that they are dangerous when left to rot in a landfill. It is estimated that there are more than 500 million used cell phones sitting around in people's homes and offices. Cell phone cases are often made of lead, which is highly toxic to all living things, and if all those 500 million phones were disposed of in landfills, they would release more than 300,000 pounds of lead. Computer monitors may contain lead, and the computer's circuit boards contain mercury, lead, and cadmium. As people switch to high-definition televisions, there will be an avalanche of old TVs crashing into our landfills, causing an amazing amount of environmental destruction.

The Environmental Protection Agency estimates that 3 million tons of e-waste is generated every year, but only 10 percent of it is recycled. (And even some of that percentage is probably shipped to third world countries, where it will be dismantled under less restrictive regulations.) It can't be dumped into a landfill and it can't be used for anything that would come into contact with food or beverages or anything people might consume. But it can be used for something like a flowerpot. So, combining graffiti art and e-waste, we launched the Urban Art Pot. We discovered a partner company that separates out the metal and turns the leftover resins into plastic that is durable and malleable, and asked them to make a few samples that the graffiti guys could hit up with their unique brand of design. The whole idea was that each pot would truly be an individual work of art.

We painted up the samples and took them to the retailers at the end of the summer in 2008. Within a month, we had orders for twenty-five thousand pots from Home Depot. So it was time to figure out how to produce this idea on a larger scale. In retrospect, I think this was the largest commercialization of unique graffiti ever undertaken. You might think that painting a lot of six-inch flowerpots is a simple matter, but since you've read this far, you know that nothing at TerraCycle ever is. Which is exactly what Steve Kachigan, who came in to take over the management of this project, found out.

The e-waste was turned into pots in California, but since the painting was going to be done by local graffiti artists, it had to be done in Trenton. The first problem was just finding the space to do it. We had a small building in the courtyard of the New York Avenue factory that we weren't doing anything with. It had been used as a garage for fixing trucks, so it was full of truck parts, including a few potentially valuable things—brand-new oil filters and air filters still in the box, which we put on eBay.

As usual, it was a race against time—the order was due at the end of December and the pots were only ordered in October. And, as usual, we didn't know exactly what would be involved in making the Urban Art Pot on a mass scale, but since we were surrounded by graffiti artists, we figured that wouldn't be a hurdle. We talked to a couple of the graffiti guys about running the entire project—managing the painting, selecting the painting equipment, the right paints, getting the rest of the graffiti crew, and whatever else had to be done. They seemed to be cool with it, until nine the first morning rolled around and they didn't show up. Turns out that a regular nine-to-five workday wasn't their thing.

With the clock ticking, we placed an ad in our local paper and hit the streets looking for more graffiti guys. Eventually, we were able to recruit ten local artists who were able to fit into our schedule and system. Our first stab at an assembly line was to put the unpaintited pots on a kind of lazy Susan, because it would be easy to turn the lazy Susan to get at all areas of the pot. We had to put on a base coat, which was a dark green, and then what we called the fade coat, a lighter green that would fade into the base coat color about halfway down the pot—the idea was that it would look like a continuous fade. Then the graffiti artists would come in and do the graffiti art on top of that. We had two people painting the base coat, and one person on the fade. After the base coat, the pots had to go through a heat tunnel to set the paint and then dry on shelves overnight.

We estimated that each person would be able to do twenty-four pots an hour, so one hundred and twenty an hour for our five painters and a thousand pots a day. That would make the order. Unfortunately, the first day was a disaster. None of the equipment worked, and it was harder to paint the pots than we figured. The lazy Susans took too long, because you had to move the pots from one lazy Susan to another so that the second coat could go on them. We probably finished fewer than one hundred pots that first day. And the second day wasn't that much better. It was clear we had a problem on our hands.

At the end of the second day, Steve called up an auto painting store, figuring that they would know something about painting on plastic, and pleaded for help. They sent down a guy named Jack. Jack was a professional car painter who was on leave from his regular job because of an injury. Jack took one look at what we'd done and said it was all wrong. That much we knew, but he also said he would fix it. In fact, not only did he offer to show us how to set up the assembly line correctly, he also said he would help manage the painting. In the painting room, Jack had us set up four tables covered with huge sheets of cardboard, which would hold twelve pots per table. He sprayed on the base coat, and when he was finished with all four, he'd go back and do the fade coat. He could paint the base coat on all forty-eight pots in half an hour. He saved the day.

On Christmas Eve, Steve got trapped in the paint room by our next-door neighbor's pit bull. This dog was vicious (a true ghetto hound) and would flip out every time you came within fifty feet of him. We've had countless TV and photo shoots in our courtyard where all you could hear was this cursed dog.

Steve was justifiably scared and had to call the police to get him out safely, but other than that everything seemed to be working out as well as we could hope.

We even had two of the graffiti guys get in a fight over something pointless. During this confrontation, one guy pulled out a knife and started threatening the other, who was saying things like, "Bring it on." Steve stepped between them, and managed to keep them apart until a deliveryman just happened to drive up. He got someone from the main office, and together they were able to keep the two graffiti guys from killing each other. We got rid of the guy with the knife, but Jack wasn't satisfied. "I've had enough of this ——," he growled, and walked out. Suddenly, our highly efficient staff was cut in half and we still had thousands of pots to paint.

Fortunately, another one of the painters, Clive, stepped into the gap. He had learned how to use all the equipment and how to do the painting, and to top it all off he had a fine arts degree from a college in Jamaica, where he's from. Steve decided that we would be able to fulfill the order with just the three of them, which he did, and on time. Clive now leads the TerraCycle painting department. The Urban Art Pot resulted in a fantastic launch at Home Depot, Fred Meyer, and a few other retailers and landed some major PR accolades from *Better Homes and Gardens* (and fifty other magazines). We recently started looking at doing holiday-themed pots—to hold poinsettias for Christmas or lilies for Easter. We even line expanded (that idea of flavoring a winning product) into a line of wastepaper basket–size trash cans. Just to pause on this one—this is one of my favorite products since it's a basket made from e-waste and covered in "waste art" to hold waste. We now even paint the used yogurt cups from the yogurt brigade, which we sell to nurseries to package their plants in. As always, once you find a way to use waste—even graffiti—there are many more opportunities than you first realized. It becomes another raw material that can be allied against many different products. What about graffiti binders?

In eco-capitalism we think of trying to make business in America more like a tree and less like a fire. A tree absorbs nutrients from the soil, the air, and the sun. Over the course of its life, it can become huge and immensely strong, but it's always returning some of what it takes. Ironically, it also survives off of the waste of other organisms—composted plant matter. As such, at the end of its life, it gradually returns to the environment much of the rest of what it has taken. Sometimes the energy it absorbs gets locked up in new forms (for instance, coal and natural gas), but it is essentially a sustainable enterprise. A fire, on the other hand, consumes resources and transforms them, using up their potential as fast as possible and typically leaving behind waste. While fires can provide some beneficial products (such as geminating seeds and renewing nature in many ways), they are not sustainable and will burn out at some point, when there's nothing left to consume.

Art, activity, and ideas in an eco-capitalist society are as much a part of the life cycle of society as anything else. We consider some things, such as graffiti, unpleasant or unattractive or offensive, and we pay to have them taken out of sight. Or sometimes, as in the case of our inner-city ghettos, we pay to move ourselves out of sight of them and forget they exist. I bet the majority of people living in Princeton (one of the wealthiest zip codes in America, and one of the whitest—for point of fact I now live there) have never walked on the streets of Trenton (one of the poorest and most dangerous zip codes in America, and one of the blackest), which is a mere ten minutes away.

Many of our cities have become blighted, their streets populated by the homeless, their economy largely based on one form of crime or another. None of this is free, however. As the authors of *Natural Capitalism* summarize it: "We pay criminals $40 billion a year for illegal drugs. Crime costs $450 billion a year. We spend $69 billion on obesity, $274 billion on heart disease and strokes, and $52 billion on substance abuse. Two generations after World War II, American cities are the ones that look bombed, while Berlin and Dresden are thriving."

Waste is a fundamental feature of the entire system, both as cause and effect. An enormous amount of time, money, and materials are required to keep the system going. In the United States, the materials used by industry amount to more than twenty times every citizen's weight every day—more than 1 million pounds per American per year. And most of that becomes waste. Ninety-five percent of a car's energy is used to move the car, and of that energy 80 percent is lost as heat and exhaust. The driver and passengers are a minor factor in the use of energy.

It is more costly to make an aluminum can than to make the soda that goes into it, but an enormous amount of the process (which takes ten months) is waste, as James Womack and Daniel Jones illustrated in their book *Lean Thinking*. Using the example of a can of soda bought in England, the process begins in Australia, where bauxite ore is mined and purified into aluminum oxide. When enough of it has accumulated, it is loaded on a giant ship and sent to Sweden or Norway (because the energy there is cheap). After a month at sea, it sits for a month or two until every ton of aluminum oxide is turned into a half ton of aluminum metal. This metal is heated to nearly 900 degrees Fahrenheit and rolled down to a thickness of an eighth of an inch. It is then rolled again, to one-eightieth of an inch. These sheets are shipped to England, where they are formed into cans, washed, dried, painted twice, lacquered, and sprayed inside with a protective coating to prevent corrosion.

These cans, topless, are then shipped to a bottler, which washes them again, fills them with soda, and seals them with a pop-top lid. The filled cans are shipped to a distributor, which ships them to stores, where they are bought by consumers. After more than three hundred days, someone buys the soda, drinks it in ten minutes, and (most of the time) throws the can in the trash. And not only the can but most of the thousands of dollars of time and energy that were invested in making it. We need to start thinking about other ways to do things.

In launching TerraCycle's lines of liquid fertilizer, cleaners, repellents, and similar products, I realized that almost all products that are sold as liquid in a bottle—from window cleaner to ant repellent—are basically water, typically 98 percent to 99 percent. No matter the brand, no matter whether it's soda or window cleaner or ant repellent, no matter whether it's eco-friendly or not. This is true even with TerraCycle products.

Bottled water was attacked in 2008 because of the waste involved in bottling and transporting something that all of us could get by walking over to the faucet and turning it on. But nobody has stopped to think that we should reinvent all the other products that have the same issues as bottled water. Personally, I think it's because consumers wouldn't want to buy concentrate and have to go to the trouble of diluting it. We could sell bottles that are empty but for a little concentrate in them. Then all the consumers have to do is fill the bottle with tap water when they get home. The lack of weight and substance will deter consumers from buying the products in this form, or at least keep them from paying current prices.

The fundamental point, however, is that we need to start thinking in new ways about what is waste and what is not. Sometimes it involves finding a new way to reuse waste, whether it's worm poop or soda bottles or graffiti art. Sometimes it demands that we start to ask questions about the real costs of the things we have in our houses (not to mention our houses themselves). Maybe we can help evolve the throwaway society into the hold-and-reuse society.

CHAPTER 14

The Art of Public Relations

Publicity has always been crucial to TerraCycle's growth. And while what we've learned about how to get publicity can be applied to any company, eco-capitalist or not, there are some unique aspects to TerraCycle and to how we got publicity over the past five years.

It wouldn't be wrong to say that TerraCycle would not exist today without publicity. That first summer, in 2002, Jon and I were just about ready to close up shop and sell the worm gin, when Suman responded to the interview we did on the radio. We were just about to run out of money again, when we won the Carrot Capital business plan contest—it wasn't their money that saved the day (since we didn't get any), it was the huge amount of publicity that came not only from winning but even more, from turning it down. Then when the Scotts suit threatened the possibility of putting us out of business, the publicity we generated with suedbyscotts.com was the biggest single factor (I think) in making them come to terms with us in a way that gave us room to grow.

Of course I'm not recommending to any small business that it turn down a heavyweight investor or try to be sued by its largest competitor, just to get press. But I am recommending that whatever happens to you, try to find the right angle to turn it into good publicity.

As I said, TerraCycle had some unique aspects that attracted publicity right from the beginning. I would never discount the importance of the words "worm poop," for instance. If we had found a way to make organic waste from Princeton's dining halls into compost super-quickly and super-cheaply, it would have been a great piece of business, but most people in the media would have put it on the stack of worthy but not exciting start-ups. "Worm poop" made everybody take notice and remember.

Of course, you can't suddenly add something unexpected and surprising to your business just to attract attention, but you can make the most of your opportunities. If we had insisted that everyone say we were making "vermicompost tea," I can't help but think we would have been dead in the water. On a side note, it did take a lot of time and convincing to get our staff to stop saying "vermicompost" and start proclaiming "worm poop." The funny thing about the term "worm poop" is that it was more or less just a TerraCycle thing and we could say it over and over again in interviews. Plus it provides for great comic relief, and most journalists aren't expecting to laugh when getting pitched. Having a good worm-poop joke or two makes our pitch fun and memorable and that makes media more interested.

While it is not the easiest thing to finesse the name TerraCycle into a radio interview countless times, it is easy with "worm poop." For example: "We take worm poop and liquefy it in our worm poop liquefaction tanks by taking solid worm poop, mixing it with water, and then letting it settle." This helps to create incredible branding—almost every article and interview about TerraCycle contains those magic words, and it makes our products recognizable in stores and on shelves.

The trick to PR is offering an interesting and timely story. Luckily, TerraCycle is both! Audiences loved the story of Marley's revival. When I dropped out of Princeton, that became part of the story, too—everyone loves being antiestablishment, and me dropping out of Princeton to sell worm poop takes the cake. You see the same thing happening with Seth Goldman at Honest Tea and Gary Erickson at Clif Bar, both of whom left their careers and started other ones. What could be better than starting a business in your mother's kitchen and living the American dream? This is a story everyone can relate to. Our Sued by Scotts campaign provided a similar attraction—people love to root for the underdog, the dropout, the comeback kid.

So from the start, TerraCycle was more than just a product, it was an intriguing and inspiring story. This heartfelt, human-interest backstory helped us get noticed by media big and small (plus a lot of hard work on our part, of course!) That's Phase 1 of the art of publicity. Everyone always said that when you launch a company you'll get press, but once that initial burst subsides, you'll need to advertise, because the marquee media like the *Wall Street Journal* won't keep writing about the same company again and again. While that's true to a certain extent, TerraCycle is living proof that there are ways to keep the media coming back for more. In five years, we have not once paid for an advertisement—and we won't—but in '07 and '08 alone, the *Wall Street Journal* has written nine articles either in the paper or on its Web site about TerraCycle.

In fact, we have seen an exponential growth in publicity in the last five years. Here are the numbers:

2003: 21 articles in media with circulation of 2.5 million
2004: 32 articles in media with circulation of 3.2 million
2005: 47 articles in media with circulation of 12.5 million
2006: 190 articles in media with circulation of 29 million
2007: 360 articles in media with circulation of 67 million
2008: 700 articles in media with circulation of over 150 million

We've done this even though it was only in 2007 that we spent as much as $100,000 on the entire publicity department (including salaries). How does a business continue to generate publicity when it is no longer the new kid on the block? What are the golden rules of attaining a growing volume of PR? And most important, how do you get the same places to keep writing about you? Here's what I've learned.

1. Do not hire a public relations firm. This is the most important rule, in my opinion, for one simple reason: PR firms are mostly in the business of getting a monthly retainer and less in the business of getting you press. If they were really in the business of getting you press, they would be paid for every article produced about a given client. The formula would be something like: "amount of space/time given to the story" times "angle taken" times "value of that space." In other words, the PR firm would earn more the longer a magazine or a television show spends on a client and the more favorably the client's core business is portrayed and the larger the audience. A brief, neutral mention in a blog would mean less. I have yet to find a PR firm that didn't hang up the phone on me after I asked them to do that.

Also, journalists—according to my friends who are journalists—strongly prefer to talk with the business owners or someone from the company instead of with an outside consultant. Journalists are always looking for an angle that no one else has found or an angle that will appeal strongly to their particular audience. Naturally, they feel they are going to get that from the company rather than from an intermediary. That leads to my next rule.

2. A press release is the story. Many journalists are overworked, and if you can give them a prepackaged story, you're golden. Most press releases are boring, long, and don't really tell a story. A product announcement, for instance, is not a story—but it could be. It is important to remember that the story is in the eye of the beholder. I'm sure that you have had a grandpa at some point go on and on (passionately, mind you) about some mundane event. Well, that's a story because your grandpa chose it to be. A killer press release is one that the publisher can print word for word if it chooses. Oh yeah, and it's all about the headline! The headline will make or break your release.

At TerraCycle, Albe Zakes has made it a rule to tailor every press release to the place it's going to. Instead of looking like a piece of boilerplate that was defrosted from the back of the freezer, it reads like a letter, beginning with a recognition of the needs, interests, and audience of the magazine or newspaper. If a release about TerraCycle Plant Food is going to the AARP magazine editor, it will talk about how senior citizens need to take special care about what chemicals are going into the house—for themselves, their pets, and their children and grandchildren. If a release is going to the *New Yorker* (just to pick a polar opposite), it will talk about how green is the new black, how the plant food is easy to use and so environmentally friendly that it will make the reader feel instantly cool.

Journalists hate to get generic, canned releases. At TerraCycle, we have mastered the art of the quick study. Take a few moments to make sure you have the right editor at the right publication and that you have a pitch perfectly oriented for their coverage area and audience. A lot of publicity departments will do that for the major media—at least they will do it in person, but TerraCycle applies the principle to everybody, small or large. As we've seen, local newspapers have been a terrific boost to TerraCycle. Which brings me to Rule 3.

3. Focus on local papers. Did you know that there are more than ten thousand local papers across America? And they are produced by a tiny number of people! They don't have enough people to cover the local baseball game or the bake sale at the local school, so they often cannot get enough local content to fill up their pages. But since the businesses in their area are their major advertisers, they are happy to provide them some space and that in turn provides TerraCycle with hundreds of local story opportunities. For example, when we launch a product at a retailer, we draft local press releases for each of the retailers' stores. Then we call the local paper in that area and tell it how a local store is carrying a cool new product—a product we deeply believe in—and voilà! There is a great chance that an article will be written.

Not only that, when we start a new brigade in a small town, we provide the newspaper not just with a description of the program and the good it does but also with pictures of schoolchildren and teachers and quotes from them about what a great thing TerraCycle is doing for the environment and the organization. It's exactly the kind of story a local newspaper values. Sure, a *Wall Street Journal* article is better for attracting investors or new clients. But most average Americans get their news from their local paper, not from national publications. So no matter if the paper has a circulation of 5,000 or 500,000, in that geographic area that paper is *the* most trusted, and often most overlooked, news source.

4. Work the phones, not the wire. Most people, once they've written their press release, feed it into the news wire and think their job is done because their story is so good. But if you really want publicity, you can't stop there. You need to call, e-mail, and keep calling. Call to make sure the press release arrived, call to see if there's anything that they need, and then call with another reason why the product is perfect for their readers. Editors and writers get hundreds of e-mails a day; they may not read your press release.

So you have to call and call until you get them on the phone. Once you're on the phone, you have to care about the story and be passionate about it in order to make them care. Also, research the writer before you call. If you're asking writers to invest time in a story about your idea, you have to invest a little in them. Make friends with the writers—if you have a good product and give them the right information, you are doing them a favor and they will remember it. Plus, always be respectful of their time and their ever-looming deadlines. Journalists have editors and publishers to make happy and deadlines to hit on a daily basis, so be aware of the constraints on their time. Always start your call by asking if they have a moment to hear a story that is perfectly suited for their "beat." If they say no, ask to schedule a better time to talk. Journalists will appreciate your awareness and consideration. If they are available to talk, then get right to the point. Journalists want a pitch that is concise and easy to understand; giving them too much information at once will only distract them and confuse your message.

5. Help the journalists do their jobs. Journalists are like most folks—they have a job and their job is to write relevant, timely, and fun articles and to make sure that those articles sell more newspapers and magazines. To do this they may need to interview lots of people around the story (which takes their time), do some research (which takes more time), and send a photographer to take some pictures (which takes more time and money). To get a journalist excited to write about you, try to help them do their job. Before you send out your press release, have quotes already prepared and interviews lined up for them, have background research available on the topic and independent analysts or experts familiar with your company and your industry, and always have high-resolution, well-shot photographs ready to go. By making the journalist's job easier, the likelihood of an article will go up and the chances of getting a longer, more robust article skyrocket. This will make journalists respect and want to work with you in the future. If they know you can supply everything they need for a solid article, they will take the time to listen to a future pitch. The challenge here is that you need to create new stories to feed to reporters who have already written about you. Every time you launch a new initiative, a new product, a new partnership, it equals press. For example, when we launched a display in OfficeMax we were able to achieve over sixty articles on that one display program.

Publicity is especially important for small companies. Ironically, big companies typically see publicity as a risk. They would prefer to control the message, which is something they can do with advertising. Publicity, which is almost by definition written by someone outside the company, becomes more risk management than positive attention. If you're a small, growing business, do not fall into that trap. Publicity is the greatest asset you have—just because you are small and growing. America is built on the American dream of starting your own business, the rags-to-riches story even when you don't have the riches yet. The media will treat you as their hero if you can demonstrate how you are fulfilling that dream. Dan Rather and CBS were willing to give us five minutes on the national evening news even when we barely had any customers. Whether you're being sued or starting a new business, publicity can be your biggest tool.

So Phase 2 is creating new stories that will keep the press interested and building relationships with the people who can make media happen for you. After that, however, the question becomes where do you go from there? How can you tap into more free and, most important, credible exposure. That's Phase 3—creating programs that drive publicity on their own. The brigades are a perfect example of that.

The best way to show how the brigades work as publicity is to imagine what the brigade looks like from the individual's point of view. Suppose ten-year-old Suzy comes home from school and tells her mother that they learned about how the earth was getting so much hotter that plants and animals are disappearing. She tells her mother sternly that they have to start recycling more. Suzy's mom agrees and suggests that a recycling project could be Suzy's fourth-grade class's community-service project.

Suzy takes the idea to school and Suzy's teacher recalls a recent article in their town newspaper about a program that encourages kids to collect used drink pouches as a way to keep them out of landfills and also as a way to raise money for her school. She tells Suzy about TerraCycle, and Suzy is excited to put this project together.

With her mom's help, Suzy goes to www.terracycle.net and sees that Capri Sun, whose juices she drinks all the time, is sponsoring an upcycling program for juice pouches—and Suzy learns that they aren't recyclable and take decades to biodegrade. Even better, the collected juice pouches are then turned into new tote bags, backpacks, and pencil cases, which are sold at major stores, including the Target her family visits every week. She's excited because, not only would her collections keep juice pouches from ending up in landfills, but also because the juice pouches are given a second life, reducing the need to produce new materials to make cool tote bags, backpacks, and other products.

Suzy clicks to the sign-up page and puts her name on the list to become a collector. Immediately, she receives an e-mail from TerraCycle saying that she can begin collecting drink pouches. Suzy tells all her friends at school, at soccer, at scouts, and at church. Even her piano teacher, whom she doesn't really like. Soon enough, every day people are giving Suzy their drink pouches. Her soccer coach even bought Capri Sun pouches for the game-day refreshments. She is in business.

Suzy opens the welcome package/shipping kit TerraCycle recently sent her. She fills the mail pouch with two hundred Capri Sun pouches, and in a few weeks Suzy logs on to her TerraCycle account page and she sees that TerraCycle has received the package of two hundred drink pouches. Suzy realizes that if she sends a package every few weeks, she can earn $20, which will feed the class hamster over the summer! In

May, the school's PTA receives a check from TerraCycle for $20, and the class hamster receives a bag of food to last him through the summer.

TerraCycle's publicity team is actively promoting the drink-pouch brigade story in Suzy's town. Local papers, blogs, school district newsletters, and even major newspapers are happy to feature what local youth, church groups, and civic clubs are doing about the waste problem. A local paper in Minnesota might not write about a New Jersey–based company, but they will put Suzy and her classmates' picture on the front cover. Articles are published daily. Over the course of a few months, many people in town have heard about this company. Naturally, Suzy's mom and many other people are curious about this company, and Suzy is happy to tell them about the worm-poop plant food and the ecologically safe cleaning products.

Suzy has not only collected thousands of juice pouches, and kept them from ending up in a landfill, but she is also a vocal advocate for the company's commitment to sustainability, and she proudly carries her school pens in a Capri Sun juice-pouch pencil case, which she recently bought at her local Wal-Mart.

But the ripple effect doesn't even end there. Multiply the attention in Suzy's town by a hundred. Now Kraft's Capri Sun brand managers are extremely pleased with the good publicity they are receiving and the sustainability department is ecstatic at the good press the company is receiving about their environmental efforts. They regularly call up the TerraCycle client service team to make requests, such as: Can TerraCycle send Kraft's board of directors tote bags for an upcoming board meeting? Can TerraCycle provide a tote bag for a rock star at a concert Capri Sun is promoting? Often, the request involves TerraCycle providing "fun facts" about upcycling to their ad agency for an upcoming TV spot dedicated to the company's sustainability programs. Conversations often lead to how the drink-pouch brigade can be further integrated into the next year's integrated marketing/communications plan.

Phase 4 is to start generating your own content. This is the key turning point, when you go from just being written about frequently to doing the writing yourself. The number of media outlets has grown dramatically over the past one hundred years, not just in form but also in numbers of each kind of media. The number of radio stations has grown in parallel with the emergence of TV, cable television, the Internet, and so on. Consequently, there is a dramatic need for content and there is not enough content available.

Moreover, as people have grown up with a medium, they have taken greater and greater control of it. Once a generation had grown up on national network television, there was a drive for more individual, more local, and more topic-specific kinds of programs. Cable television filled that need and people began making their own television programs. The invention of the handheld video camera made it possible for almost anyone to produce a television show. The number of talk shows, reality shows, and call-in shows increased dramatically.

The Internet has brought this spread of media and of individually produced media to its zenith. There is a big opportunity to start creating your content. This can be as simple as starting to write your own blog—most businesses have their own blogs these days. Once you become the creator of the content, you can become the expert and be invited onto shows for your expertise in the subject. For example, Wendy Bounds, a reporter who was our first contact with the *Wall Street Journal,* has a weekly show on CNBC to discuss her specialty, small business.

TerraCycle's natural home was the Internet. Bloggers have always loved TerraCycle, and when the Scotts suit hit, articles about it swirled all over the Internet. There were hundreds of articles that we actually pitched to the bloggers. They don't get many stories pitched to them, so they were extremely receptive and love getting pitch calls and e-mails. The blogs are mainly concerned about gathering material. They're not restricted by space—so they can run as many articles as they want—and what they really want is material that will drive traffic to their site to keep their advertisers happy and so that they will get more Google ad dollars. The more the better, as far as they're concerned.

The big realization came to me after *Inc.* magazine, which had written seven articles about TerraCycle, contacted me about writing a blog for them. I had written a piece about the Scotts suit for their Web site, and at the beginning of 2008 they were starting several new blogs. They asked if I would write about eco-capitalism. I began with a post called "The Secret Formula for Generating Crazy Amounts of PR." Don't worry about looking it up; you're reading it.

Which is exactly my point. Writing that blog made me start to think about how to further leverage what I was writing. It became apparent to me that once you've been written about enough, the next phase is to become the content. After years of getting articles in the *Wall Street Journal* and the *New York Times,* TerraCycle itself has become an expert, an entity respected enough to offer its own opinion on current events or the green movement. Especially in the Internet era, where there are thousands of sites dedicated to certain industries, all in need of good content.

Most of you reading this book are generally familiar with the sites whose purpose is to enable people to share content that they think is important or interesting, or just weird. Places like Digg.com or Reddit.com or hugg.com, which is the green version of Digg.com. So we could post my *Inc.* magazine piece on five of the content-sharing sites. If one person on each site writes about it on their own blog and links to the original *Inc.* posting, you have eleven hits. So bloggers syndicate themselves by posting their own articles on the sharing sites, making them available to hundreds of thousands of people by posting them on Digg.com and the other sites. And these people might link to it on their site. As I say, the more content the better.

So I decided that we needed more blogs—not on our Web site, but on other sites, which makes the content much more credible and much more likely to be picked up by others. Since each Web site wants original content, we drew up a list of the different subjects we could write about from an expert point of view. We decided to pitch blogs about business, eco-business, packaging, and the environment. We have a couple of major Web sites that are very interested, and if two or three agree, we will have a major Internet success. By the time this book is published, the TerraCycle blog will be syndicated in over thirty blogs and we may have columns in a number of magazines.

This book falls into Phase 4. You may have bought the book in the first place because you heard about TerraCycle on the radio or read about us in the newspaper. The publication of the book creates more publicity, and that publicity will generate more sales and more brigades, which will generate more publicity. TerraCycle is also in the midst of filming a TV show, which will start its own cycle of generating publicity.

The ultimate goal is Phase 5, where you or your business is watched by the media, and therefore by the public, so that anything you do publicly (and all too often privately) becomes part of the news cycle. In a word, you have reached the point of being a celebrity, and that has become a very powerful force in today's media-driven world. Becoming famous drives massive free media which, as Bono and others have effectively noted, can be directed to generate awareness and momentum for good.

CHAPTER 15

How to Launch an Eco-Friendly Product Every Week

Our new factory in Trenton has an entire floor that is enclosed in chain-link fence that is under lock and key. Yet everything that comes onto that floor is waste. What's going on? Ironically, the only difference between our warehouses and a landfill is that in one waste is separated and in the other it is completely mixed.

The answer is that everything behind those fences is pristine, preconsumer branded waste. It may be the most valuable waste in the world. Of course all of it is either slightly wrong or slightly old or somehow a problem for Kraft or Frito-Lay or the others. Imagine if this waste got into the wrong hands? Packaging inferior candies, chips, or cookies in these high-quality, high-profile brands' wrapping paper would not only be a rip-off on the consumer but a black eye for the brand's owner. So we've made sure the security is airtight.

Our partnership with Kraft and other larger corporations suddenly provided us with a flood of riches, or at least riches of waste. Because of the size of these companies, even that one-tenth of 1 percent that is misprinted or out of date provides us with an enormous quantity of raw material. Since we didn't want it to go to waste, we took aggressively to product expansion.

That's noticeably less problematic for TerraCycle than for a major corporation that follows the standard model of product development. When a large company decides to bring a completely new product to market, they know that they are embarking on a long and complicated process—which may not even be a success. Even apart from large, complicated products like an automobile or a washing machine, a company can spend years and millions of dollars introducing a new product—obstacles that naturally make them very careful about trying anything new.

They begin by identifying an unaddressed consumer need that falls within their brand. That involves market research either by the in-house staff or by consultants, and can involve interviews and focus groups. Lots of time and money. Then they have their designers or engineers develop responses to the consumer need they've identified, and that inevitably involves several departments, lots of meetings, and perhaps even new research into materials or ingredients. More time and money. Ultimately, they narrow it down to one or sometimes two new products that they test with consumers, sometimes by giving away samples and making surveys of the users.

If the tests are successful, they then have to build up their production infrastructure, so that they know they will be able to manufacture the large numbers of the product that will have to go out if the new thing is a hit with the consumer. The last thing a big company wants is to be out of stock of a hot new item. This may involve retooling a factory or hiring new people or both. At the same time, the sales, marketing, and publicity people are putting together a plan that is intended to get the product off the shelves of the retailers (who don't yet know anything about it). This itself takes time and money, and it is also a plan that will call for more enormous amounts of time and money to be spent—if all goes well.

This process can cost as much as $10 million and take up to two years. It also locks the company into the product, even though it may fail. Often, if the initial results are disappointing, the company then puts even more money into promoting the product, offering discounts, advertising more heavily, and on and on. The potentially vicious cycle can truly be a waste.

We flipped this process on its head. To do this we made a couple of global assumptions. First, that customers would always rather buy an eco-friendly choice if it is available (that is, they don't have to go out of their way to find it), and especially if it is not priced more than a comparative product that is not eco-friendly. That seemed a safe assumption based on our experience and on what we saw around us.

The second major assumption is that the big retailers know what their customers want. This seemed a safe assumption since they know what sells in their stores. In fact, we went a step further than that. Because the major retailers attract such a large percentage of consumer spending, we thought it was reasonable to figure that what the big retailers want is what consumers in general want. Even if someone doesn't shop at Target or Home Depot, we thought it was still likely that consumers would be interested in a product that had broad enough appeal to be a success at these big-box stores.

That second assumption was the basis for another revolutionary business model that TerraCycle has pioneered, at least pioneered as our primary way of determining which products we will work on next. We call what we have invented "discovery selling." That is, our product development actually begins, as often as not, with our sales force.

Typically, companies only visit one buyer at each retailer they see. For instance, as a plant food company, we only saw the buyer in the lawn and garden department at our retail partners. And for the most part, sales reps are selling a preexisting line of products. So sales reps walk into the meeting having already determined what product they are going to pitch. If they have a new product, they might bring along a prototype of it, but remember that their company has already put a substantial amount of money into developing not only the product but the internal resources necessary to rolling out that product in a big way. In other words, what they offer is not flexible—the buyers can't suggest changes.

Once the reps explain the new product and why it will be attractive to consumers, they pull out what is probably the most important thing to the buyer: a marketing plan. A marketing plan has a number of aspects, but what they all come down to in the end is: $$$. Typically, the plan will include television ads, radio ads, print advertising, Web advertising, and perhaps product giveaways, promotional prices, store coupons, in-store promotional pieces, and so on. There will also be a plan about how they will attract publicity for the product, which might be product reviews in newspapers or mentions in "what's-new" columns in magazines or the like. As far as the company (and the store) is concerned, publicity is just advertising they didn't pay for. But of course, all of that publicity involves sending out free samples of the product and the enormous amount of literature that will accompany it. You get the idea though—millions of dollars.

Finally, the salespeople will talk about a price for the product and suggest how many of it the buyer should order. Buyers may bargain a bit on both of these figures, but essentially it's a take-it-or-leave-it proposition. Although the big-box stores have real impact on the large consumer-product companies, those companies also control a very large and diverse array of products that go into the stores. Basically, everybody wants to maintain good relations, so they will tend to come to an agreement that is satisfactory to both sides.

The TerraCycle model is completely different. When one of our sales reps meets a buyer for the first time, they start out by telling the buyer about TerraCycle. We give them a presentation about the history of the company—how it was founded and how it has built a business paradigm based on waste streams. We point out how that concept allows us to make cool products, products unlike anything else on the market, that are cost-effective at the same time. We describe the brigades—that we collect waste in schools and churches, which use the money they earn for charity or another community benefit.

Then we show them how the media reacts to the things we do: some of the television shows that have done stories on us, a clip from the show *The Big Idea,* and a preview of the TerraCycle television show that will be on National Geographic Television in 2009. Finally, we show them specific examples of our products—the pencil cases, backpacks, and the like. It's very interactive—often our salesperson doesn't even talk about specific products for the store until the very end.

For example, our vice president of sales, Dave Campodonico, was going into meetings at Wal-Mart in spring 2008 when his cell phone rang. The call was from a Wal-Mart buyer of home products who was actually in the building. He said, "You guys are the buzz of the building right now, and I hear that it's pretty interesting. I'd like to meet with you." This is unheard of, by the way—buyers don't usually make the call to sales reps. But Dave arranged a time, and the buyer showed up with another person from home products, and a third person, really just a spectator who was interested in seeing what TerraCycle was all about. Dave made pretty much the presentation I just described and showed some examples of our fused materials. The buyer looked them over and said, "Well, I'd like to see what you could do with a shower curtain. I think it would be great for back-to-school if you could do it with chip bags or cookie bags or something like that."

So without having the faintest idea he would be selling shower curtains that day, Dave suddenly found himself at the starting point of a new product development cycle.

Whenever we start on a new project, we follow a few basic golden rules:

1. Do not invent a new form of the product, just reinvent it in a more eco-friendly way, if at all possible from waste.

2. Leverage your raw materials. When you look at garbage and isolate a stream (for example, drink pouches), look at what it can be used for as a material. Drink pouches can be sewn together, creating the possibility for hundreds of products, all coming from one waste stream.

3. Keep the price competitive with any similar product on the market. In fact, we've never had any problems with pricing, largely because our raw materials are so cheap and our marketing budget so small.

4. Make sure it has the same (or more, or better) features, benefits, and efficacy as any similar product.

5. Keep it simple, especially when it comes to technology and regulation. Keep the products simple (no moving parts, no complicated electronics, and so on). Even with these limits the potential is massive with thousands of products.

6. Stay away from regulatory headaches. Some products are ridiculously highly regulated (for example, plant food, which requires that you certify your labels in every state), while other products (for example, cleaners) are unregulated and require no such headaches. If a regulator says no to your product, it can screw up a national launch faster than anything.

In discovery selling, we don't profess to know everything about a category or a product—what the price points are, what the demographics are, what the geographic distribution would be, or things like that. We just say we have a bunch of waste that we can throw together to make cool-looking products. Wal-Mart also asked us to create a messenger bag—the design process involved going to Wal-Mart, buying a few Hannah

Montana messenger bags, and sending them to our designers with a note that says, "Hi! Make this out of juice pouches or whatever makes sense."

With the messenger bags, we mocked up some samples, and then had a series of meetings with the Wal-Mart buyers. They were involved in every part of it—the structure, the color, the stitching. After six or seven meetings, they agreed to test market them in fifty stores in New Jersey. The shower curtain was the same—the result of joint discussions between the merchant and Dave. We wound up making it out of Oreo cookie wrappers, and the finished curtains were shipped at the end of August '08.

There are several perhaps unexpected benefits to this kind of product development. First, the retailer becomes very invested in the product. The more time they spend with the process, the more it becomes what they want and the more likely they are to buy it. In fact, we've never been turned down at the end of the process—our success rate is 100 percent.

In addition, once we shifted our focus from being a plant food company to a company that sells products made from waste, we could hugely expand the possibilities of what we could sell. Combined with discovery selling, which means that we can work with the store to create products, it means that our salespeople are not limited to a single buyer within a company, or even a group of related buyers. When we're dealing with Wal-Mart or Target, we can meet with any buyer that deals with home or office products.

At the beginning of the year, I constantly reminded the salespeople that they should be working to have more meetings with more buyers across the board. Well, "reminded" would not be the word they used, but the effect has been fantastic. Dave visits Bentonville, Wal-Mart's headquarters, every two weeks, but it's not often enough anymore. As Dave says, "It's a little like drinking out of a fire hose. You just hope that what is sliding off the side of your face isn't that important. It's not for the faint of heart."

Once we had the discovery selling model down, we developed another approach to selling that complemented discovery selling: "360-degree selling." Retailers review certain products during certain times of the year, usually nine to twelve months before the actual selling season—Christmas products in January, lawn and garden during the summer, back to school and stationery during October, and so forth. These are the only times they will see you. So when all we sold was plant food we had our sales meetings during one month of the year. The rest of the year we were out of luck—and sometimes out of money.

But now that we had become a company that could make so many different products—in fact, there is no limit on how many products we could make—we could and should be in sales meetings year-round. So we created a calendar of sales seasons and noticed that something is always being reviewed. All we needed to do was to invent products that fit every season.

With this approach to selling, we have relatively little investment into our new products prior to seeing their performance on the shelf, so if it doesn't sell we move on to the next thing. As a result, we've grown from having perhaps a dozen different products to more than a hundred, in less than two years.

Some of that growth comes from "flavoring" our existing products that are already doing well. We discovered with the plant food that there was very little fundamental difference between a general-purpose plant food and, for instance, a plant food specifically for orchids. Just a bit of tweaking was all we needed to put out a new product, and when we did, our sales increased noticeably. Flavoring is a way consumer-product companies play human psychology. People prefer to have specific products for specific functions. They feel sure it will work better even though it's the same product.

No one who walks down any aisle of a supermarket these days will be surprised at what I'm saying—for instance, there is a cleaning product for every different surface in your house.

You can buy a bathroom cleaner, a toilet bowl cleaner, a shower cleaner, and a tile cleaner, a cooktop cleaner, a stainless steel cleaner, a glass cleaner, and an eyeglass cleaner. But how much real difference is there between them? Very little—the active ingredients are for the most part the same in all of them—the only significant differences are in scent and color. Since companies are not required to list the ingredients unless their product might come into contact with food (or be eaten itself), it's hard to know.

As I became aware of how much you could do with other people's garbage, I became hyperaware of everything around me and what its life cycle was. You can do this exercise yourself: wherever you are, simply look at each object around you in turn and try to imagine what will happen to it at the end of its life. There's probably a chair, a carpet, a window, curtains and curtain rods, a lamp, a cord, a shade, and a lightbulb. Now think about what happens to these things when you (or whoever owns them) no longer wants them. You can probably think of various outcomes. Most of them will eventually lead to a landfill or an incinerator, but the point is that every product, every thing, has an end of life. And that's where TerraCycle comes in.

The thing with making products out of waste—when you're talking about the kinds of quantities that Target or another large store will order—is that you need a lot of any specific kind of waste and you need to be able to depend upon your source for it. So I began to evaluate things around me in terms of what happened to them at their end of life, and how much of them I could get my hands on. I thought about circuit boards, since electronics have become a throwaway item in our society, and most of their parts are not recyclable. Unfortunately, these are very hard to find. Although there are plenty of manufacturing screwups, no company wants to admit to them, so preconsumer waste is hard to find. Postconsumer boards can be found, but by then components have been soldered on and it's difficult to remove them. However, the containers—the monitor housings, the CPU boxes, printer cases—can be used.

I also thought about the pull tabs that are pulled off aluminum drink cans and litter our streets. The pull tabs are actually the most valuable part of the can for recyclers, since they are pure aluminum, unlike the rest of the can. They are very specialized items, so we decided to partner with people already looking at this waste stream. In this case it's the Ronald McDonald House, which collects pull tabs nationally.

Hundreds of millions of CDs and DVDs are discarded every year by the industry—either albums or games or videos that haven't sold or disks that were overprints. The numbers are astonishing, even a little sickening. The companies won't give them to us unless we prove that we will destroy them, so the solution was to laser cut the discs into Christmas ornaments.

Vinyl billboards are very strong and nonrecyclable—and millions are thrown out every year. They can be sewn into fantastic products, but are hard to access because of the intellectual property that is printed on them. We recently worked out an agreement with Coca-Cola to upcycle their billboards.

One of the reasons for our success is that there hasn't been any direct competition in this field, even though the environment has become one of the hottest fields. Today there are fundamentally two types of companies trying to make eco-friendly products: big companies that operate on the traditional capitalist model and small companies that operate on what you might call the environmental profit model. The former focus more on price but not environmental innovation; the later, on environmental impact but charge a premium for their products.

Big companies have great distribution, but they also have a major infrastructure already in place. Even when they decide to make an eco-friendly product they need to stay within the same method of product development. This usually means that they integrate recycled content into their packaging and slightly change the contents of the product—in both cases the change is typically minimal. With such a large preexisting infrastructure, they have a very hard time reinventing how their product is made so that it may be maximally eco-friendly.

The small companies operating on the environmental model generally focus on small retailers and price their products at the high end. Because their products are significantly more expensive, they have a very hard time selling to the big-box stores—even if they want to, which they often don't. The result is that they are limited to the minor leagues of American retail.

TerraCycle got its start in big-box stores and has relied on them for growth. Discovery selling and 360-degree selling can only work in the big-box environment, because only those stores can place an order that would financially justify the cost of figuring out how to make a new product from scratch. They also offer fantastic access to sales data (as opposed to no access at all with small retailers), prompt payment, and credibility. Perhaps most importantly, the population that shops in big-box retailers is not the majority of Americans, but tends to be those less informed and focused on environmental issues.

As of today, the combination of discovery selling and 360-degree selling has been fantastically successful. Within a year, TerraCycle launched over one hundred products ranging from winter (fire logs to ice melt), holiday (bows to ornaments), cleaning (drain cleaner to window cleaner), lawn and garden (composters to deer repellent), and office (binders to pencil cases), bags (computer bags to shopping bags) to home (frames to shower curtains). Because of this process, we are now launching nationally an environmentally friendly product made from waste every week, and our timeline from concept to store shelf averages six months (in contrast to the two-year cycle of most companies). Is it possible to continue such massive, perpetual product expansion? Given the environmental need and consumer demand for better and cheaper green products, I believe it is.

CONCLUSION

Eliminating the Idea of Waste

The idea that inspired me in 2001 in a basement in Montreal has fostered one of the fastest-growing and groundbreaking private companies in America. I'm excited by TerraCycle's momentum and potential, but for me, the goal isn't growth for growth's sake but rather growth to reduce—or even eliminate—the very substance on which our business is based: waste.

One of the reasons I've been fascinated by waste it that it defies the standard parameters of typical supply-and-demand economics. Go to Google and search for images of "supply demand curve" and you will find hundreds of examples of "price" (beginning at zero) on the vertical axis and "quantity" (also beginning at zero) on the horizontal axis. Basically, the curves show that prices increase as supply goes down and the converse, but I have yet to find a "supply-demand" curve that focuses on what happens in the negative. In other words, the concept of "negative demand," taking into account the price someone would pay to dispose of an item.

Waste is simply any commodity that we are willing to pay to get rid of. It is the only commodity in the world that has true negative value. Waste exists partly because of economics, because in many cases it is cheaper to throw something out than to reuse it or properly recycle it, and companies have yet to be required to maintain responsibility for the entire life cycle of their products. Many major companies have now voluntarily contracted for sponsored waste programs with TerraCycle, taking responsibility for their packaging waste in cooperation with their consumers who collect it.

So what happens if TerraCycle grows and creates more and more demand for waste? What happens if other companies do the same? As with any commodity, when demand increases, the price for it goes up. So if waste starts at negative $50 per ton (that is, that's what people will pay to get rid of it), increased market demand for that waste would drive the price up to negative $40, then negative $30. With more and more demand, the price would continue to increase—that is, be less negative. Eventually, there would come that magical moment when the price would go above $0 and become positive. At that moment, the commodity has stopped being waste.

I know, we're a long way away from eliminating waste, but my goal is to turn a vicious cycle into a virtuous one. And speaking about virtue, I often get asked about whether TerraCycle is just allowing some big corporations to greenwash, since they continue to produce tons upon tons of packaging (and many people object to what they put in the packages and to some of their other business practices). I can't say that I agree with the corporate policies of all of the companies TerraCycle works with, but we're here to help solve a huge environmental problem—waste—and I can assure you, the corporations we work with and the people who work in them are very committed to addressing this problem, in large part because their consumers have made it clear that they prioritize the issue. It is those same consumers, though, who demand the convenience of disposable packaging; the manufacturers and retailers are responding to their consumers when they produce these countless tons of packaging.

Right now, TerraCycle is offering for nonrecycled packaging the only scalable solution other than landfills. If we are going to truly change the cycle of creating this waste, a change in consumer patterns is essential. Think about everything you have purchased in the past month. Almost all of it will become waste in a year or two, and statistically 99 percent of it becomes waste in a period of six months. Billions of dollars are spent each year hauling our waste out of sight, and most waste-management companies are principally haulers, as there is no management of waste. And, the waste we see, municipal solid waste, is only 1 to 2 percent of the total waste generated by processes. I don't claim to have the answer other than to say that I remain intrigued by the question of how to reverse the cycle of waste creation, and I know part of the answer lies with the consumer and part lies in manufacturers treating as assets what they now regard as liabilities.

The TerraCycle story doesn't end here, but this book does. I hope you are looking forward to the sequel as much as I am. The company isn't a start-up anymore, but we are just beginning to have a meaningful impact. As an example, in the first eight months of 2008, TerraCycle and the people participating in its brigades have kept 52 million juice pouches, 5 million energy bar wrappers, 1 million soda bottles, and 10 million cookie wrappers from ending up in landfills, a small fraction of the billions that did. I've no doubt TerraCycle will greatly scale up its efforts and impact, and thus scale down the amount of wasted waste. What's most intriguing to me is how the business model will evolve. I have no doubt there will be more than a few twists as the journey unfolds.

Cheers,
Tom

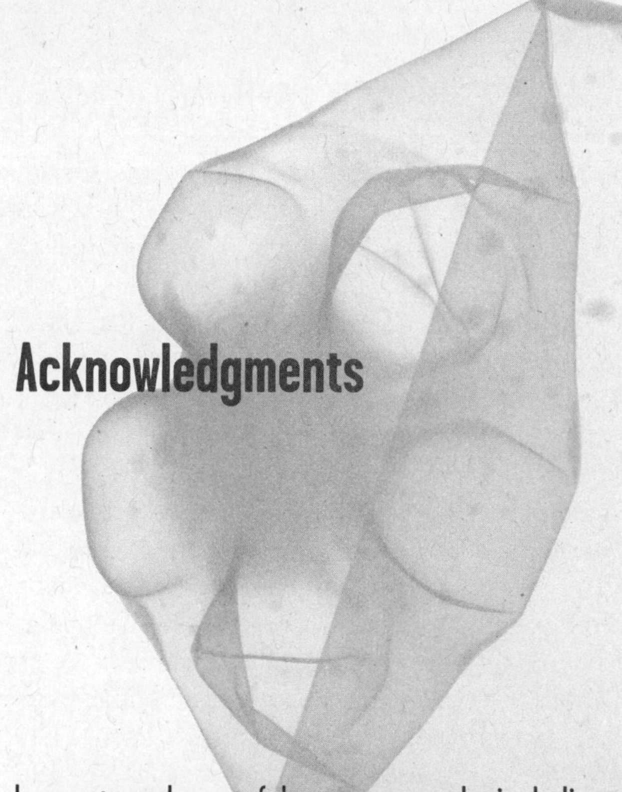

Acknowledgments

I am extremely grateful to many people, including some I don't know personally, who have believed in TerraCycle and who have helped with its formation and growth over the years.

My first acknowledgment is to Soyeon, my wife and tireless partner in life and the ever-evolving TerraCycle journey; to her sister, Soeun; and to our parents and extended family. With the deepest love and thanks for everything—large and small—and for the irreplaceable gift of patience.

To the folks who believed in me and the vision for TerraCycle from the very beginning and who took the greatest risks to be a part of this dream: Robin, Bill, Jon, Noemi, Ryan, Stu, Hilary, Alex, Steve, Brian, Sam, and to many others who were there but are not here mentioned. To the folks at the Eco-Complex: Dr. Janes, Russle, Dr. Joe, Dave, Priscilla, and the rest of the team for providing critical help when no one else would.

To the over 150 interns who have spent their summers

working at TerraCycle, for helping to drive the dream and constantly push the envelope.

To the TerraCycle management and labor teams, including the more than sixty people currently employed at TerraCycle who work every day to translate the dream into reality. Thank you Betsy, Sheryl, Donna, Jared, Elaine, Cokey, Fred, Dave, Ellen, Brian, Robin, Ron, Dara, Dean, Wendy, Pat, Larry, Milton, the Steves and the Michaels, Joel, Dr. Joe, Dr. Bill, Pierre, Lawrence, Kevin, Theresa, Tiffany, Albe, George, Dan, Chris, Ed, James, Richard, all those not mentioned, those that came before, and those that will join us soon. Also, great thanks to our indirect labor in Mexico, Canada, California, and across the world for their important contribution to our work.

To the many investors who believed in us and the evolving vision for TerraCycle, with particular thanks to Edith and Martin Stein, Victor and Antonio Elmaleh, John, Rich, Dave, Josh, Suman, AAI, Investors Circle, Phil, Good Works Ventures, Renewal Partners, Fulcrum, Peak Ventures, InvestEco, Nora, Duncan, Jon, Ken, Steve, Ron, Sean, Niko, Perlins, Gilliams, Jeff, Joan, Kathleen, Isles, Josh, Doug, David, Andy, Fran, Brett, and those not mentioned above.

To our advisors and past and current board members: Enoch, Tom, Rich F., Rich S., Royce, Phil, and Mary for your advice even when it hasn't been easy to give.

To our sponsored waste and retail partners, and the people within those organizations for enabling and taking a risk with TerraCycle, especially Wes, Mary, Reggie Jonaitis, Bill Bonner, Ron Jerutis, Dick Arnold, Jack Abelarde, Tony Romero, Sally Mueller, Rand Waddoups, Ryan McCoy, Steve Yucknut, Jeff Chahley, Vinay Sharma, Fran Hinckley, Carly Lutz, Erik Drake, Jessica Chau, Ryan Therriault, the folks at Honest Tea, Clif Bar, Stonyfield, Kraft Foods, Frito-Lay, Starbucks, Bare Naked, Kashi, J&J, Home Depot, Wal-Mart, Target, Office Max, Kroger, Petco, Fred Meyer, Whole Foods, Sams Club, Shop Rite, Zellers, Menards, Walgreens, CVS, RiteAid, and the many others.

To everyone in Toronto who helped form my perspectives, Anthony, Jake, Dan, Blakley, Pete, Victor Verblac, Paul, Mary and Tom Boyle, and Jim Budman.

To the folks in the media who helped spread the word on TerraCycle, especially Bo Burlingham, Wendy Bounds, James Baggett and the Meredith Team, Matt Bennett and the Silent Crow Crew, Paul Frank and the team at The Firm, Daryl Hannah, The Lazy Environmentalist, and to everyone else who has written about TerraCycle.

To the vast community of environmental organizations and to the millions of individuals who have championed the environment over the past few decades, for inspiration and for creating the awareness in consumers', producers', and retailers' minds and hearts through which a company like TerraCycle could take hold and thrive.

To the team at Penguin, especially Courtney Young and Adrian Zackheim, and Alan Nevins at The Firm.

To nature, for teaching me that there is no waste, only an input for some other process or creature, and especially to the worms, whose peaceful and industrious ways provided the original inspiration for TerraCycle.

And finally, to the millions of people who participate in TerraCycle's brigades and who buy our products. Your daily actions demonstrate the cumulative power of many small steps toward a better world.